'Rise 'N' Shine: Catholic Education and the African-American Community

Mary Alice Chineworth, OSP

Editor

National Catholic Educational Association

ISBN 1-55833-177-8

Dedication

To the cherished memory of the Most Rev. James P. Lyke, archbishop of Atlanta, who shortly before his death forcefully reminded us that "Catholic education is the lifeblood of evangelization."

Isaiah: 60:1
"Arise, be enlightened, for thy light has come..."
Traditional spiritual based on Isaiah: 'Rise, Shine; for thy light is a-coming'...

TABLE OF CONTENTS

FOREWORD

I am delighted and greatly honored to have been invited to write the foreword to this publication, *'Rise 'n' Shine: Catholic Education and the African-American Community.* This scholarly publication is long overdue. Forty-four years ago, when I enrolled as a graduate student at the Catholic University of America, I was dismayed to find no African-American professors or scholars engaged in writing and teaching about the role that Catholic education had played in the formation and education of thousands of African Americans as far back as the eighteenth century. Courageous religious women and men, along with dedicated lay persons, established schools for the newly freed slaves. They did so without approval of many church leaders and in some instances against their opposition. These early Catholic educators included African-American sisters and priests, who built on the foundations laid during the terrible periods of enslavement. We know that many African slaves took the Bible as their deliverance book and found that God in America, whom they may have known only in a shadowy form.

While at Catholic University I became convinced that what was needed now were African-American women and men who would build upon the foundation and tradition of Catholic education provided by the Church, and by study, reflection and scholarly research, reveal to the Church and the world what African Americans had contributed and continue to contribute to education in general and, more specifically, to Catholic education.

The journey has been long, but much has been accomplished. We now have African-American religious, priests and lay people, who are eminent scholars, capable not only of speaking to the role of Catholic education in the African-American community but also in a much broader context, and who have played a major role in helping all of us to understand how African Americans have impacted on that education. One might say that our African-American Catholics are providing heady new wine and have the new wineskins in which to place that wine.

The authors of this book bring us to an expanded view of what we and our African ancestors have seen and heard.

Most Rev. Joseph A. Francis, SVD
Rted. Auxiliary Bishop of Newark

CONTRIBUTING AUTHORS AND EDITOR

Sister Mary Alice Chineworth, OSP
Editor

A member of the Oblate Sisters of Providence since 1936, Sister Mary Alice was born in Rock Island, Illinois, and received her education (K through 12) in St. Joseph School there. Subsequently she earned a B.A. in English from Mount Mary College in Milwaukee and an MA and PhD from The Catholic University of America. After 20 years in the teaching ministry in schools of the order, she assumed editorial responsibility for Oblate News and Views, a publication of the community. She presently serves as director of ongoing formation and resides at the motherhouse in Baltimore, Maryland.

Beverly A. Carroll

Beverly A. Carroll is the founding Executive Director of the Secretariat for Black Catholics of the National Conference of Catholic Bishops. Prior to her appointment in 1988, she served the Urban Church in the Archdiocese of Baltimore in various capacities beginning as clerk-typist and progressed to Executive Director of the Office of Urban Affairs. The Baltimore native earned a Bachelor's degree in Administration from the University of Maryland and a Masters in Liberal Arts from Towson State University. She has held many positions, including Secretary of the National Association of Black Catholic Administrators, and Administrator of Lawrence Cardinal Shehan Scholarship Fund. She received the 1988 Woman of the Year Award from Zeta Phi Beta Sorority, Inc. and Martin Luther King Award for work in civil rights. She was the Archdiocesan Ambassador to the Eucharistic Congress in Nairobi, Kenya. She has served on the Paulist Board of Evangelization, the Board of Trustees for the Chicago Theological Union, the Holy Name Province of Franciscans' African American Committee, and currently serves on the Advisory Committee for the Institute for Black Catholic Studies at Xavier University of Louisiana. She is the producer of "The Cypress will Grow" a video for evangelization in the African American community. Past accomplishments include Editor of filmstrips: "Unraveling the Evangelical Cord" and "If Rivers Could Speak," past President of the Fr. Charles A. Hall Cluster School, and participant in Black Womens' Exchange Program sponsored by the British Council of Churches.

DR. JOSEPH A. BROWN, SJ

Formerly the director of the Institute for Black Catholic Studies at Xavier University of Louisiana, Fr. Brown has taught at the University of Virginia and Creighton University. He received a Ph.D. in American Studies from Yale University, and an MA in Black Studies, also from Yale. In addition, he received an MA from the writing seminars at Johns Hopkins University . Fr. Brown has published his poetry in various magazines and anthologies. A collection of his poems, "Accidental Grace" was Volume 6 of the Callaloo Poetry Series. He writes and lectures on issues concerning black theology, literature and philosophy and is a liturgical consultant to various groups in the black Catholic Church in the United States.

DR. LORETTA M. BUTLER

Dr. Butler, associate professor emeritus at Roosevelt University in Chicago, is presently a consultant and researcher for black history projects. She received her BS from Miner Teachers College, and her MA and PhD from The Catholic University of America. Dr. Butler served as Professor of Education at Xavier University of Louisiana and as Associate Professor of Education at Columbia University. She has over twenty-five years of experience as a principal and teacher in public and Catholic schools in New Orleans and Washington, DC. She has written and lectured extensively on racial justice and Catholic action.

DR. GILES A. CONWILL

Giles A. Conwill earned a PhD from Emory University in Cultural Studies (African American history and cultural anthropology). He also holds a Master of Divinity degree from the Atheneum of Ohio with an emphasis in systematic theology. His BA in Philosophy is from the University of San Diego. Dr. Conwill's scholarly interests and research are primarily in the area of cultural and religious history of African Americans. Presently, an associate professor in the history department of Morehouse College, Dr. Conwill has published articles and chapters on black Catholic history, evangelization, religious education, preaching, liturgy, and black music. He is also on the summer faculty of Xavier University's Graduate Institute for Black Catholic Studies in New Orleans, and the Black Catholic Congress' Ministerial Training Program in Washington, D.C. Dr. Conwill also served for 14 years as an ordained Roman Catholic priest in parishes in San Diego and Atlanta, and served for four years as director of the department of church vocations for the National Office for Black Catholics in Washington, D.C.

SISTER EVA REGINA MARTIN, SSF

Sister Eva Regina, a sister of the Holy Family, is a graduate of the Institute for Black Catholic Studies at Xavier University of Louisiana. She is currently a doctoral candidate at Temple University. Sister Eva has been published in the following: *Plenty Good Room,* a liturgy training publication for African-American Catholics, *In a Word* and *Signs of Soul.* Sister Eva has been a principal and teacher for many years in schools Louisiana and Texas. She has also been a resource teacher to schools in Dangriga, Central America. Her specialization is religion and culture.

THERESE WILSON FAVORS

Ms. Wilson Favors is the Director of African American Catholic Ministry for the Archdiocese of Baltimore. She has also served as the Coordinator of Elementary and Family Catechesis for the Archdiocese and as Director of Evangelization and Community Outreach for Corpus Christi Church in Baltimore, Maryland. Ms. Wilson Favors has extensive experience as an educator in both Catholic schools and parish religious education programs. She served on the Advisory Board of the United States Catholic Conference - National Conference of Catholic Bishops from 1973-76 and as Adjunct Professor for the Desalles School of Theology.

Ms. Wilson served as Executive Director of the National Black Catholic Congress. She is the co-author of two filmstrips " Unraveling the Evangelical Cord" and "Black Catholic Identity—If Rivers Could Speak." Her articles have been published in *Today's Catholic Teacher* and *Paulist Press* and she is the author of over 100 bible study booklets for African American youth. She is the author of the *Rise Up and Rebuild Program,* a cultural and spiritual family based program for African Americans and editor of *God Bless Them Who Have Their Own: African American Catechetical Camp Meetin' Proceedings.* Ms. Wilson Favors conducts workshops for schools and parishes on the topics of religious education and evangelization from an African American perspective.

INTRODUCTION

Our Catholic community in this country has always been singularly blessed with the presence of people from many cultures, with successive waves of immigrants from Europe and Asia adding their traditions to those of the native peoples who had already marked centuries of living on this land. In days past and in our own time, escape from poverty and oppression and a search for freedom and opportunity were the motivating forces which lured many immigrants to our shores. Many others, however, were forcefully snatched from their homelands and their families and brought here against their will. These, our African-American brothers and sisters, brought with them a richness of tradition, arts, and spirituality which could have been destroyed but instead were both deepened and strengthened by the trauma and suffering experienced in this land of ours. It is important that all American Catholics understand and appreciate these gifts of beauty, courage, and faith which so enrich our Church and our nation today.

For African Americans generally, and African-American Catholics in particular, quality education has always been among the highest priorities. For this reason, NCEA is proud to present the views of these outstanding educational leaders.

Catherine McNamee, CSJ
President, NCEA

ACKNOWLEDGEMENTS

'*R*ise 'n' Shine is the product of a collaborative effort of a number of African-American educators, historians and pastoral ministers from a variety of institutional settings.

Special thanks to Ms. Beverly Carroll, Executive Director of the Secretariat for African-American Catholics, National Conference of Catholic Bishops, for her ongoing encouragement and support.

We are especially indebted to the African-American educators who took the time out of their busy schedules to participate in the focus groups that helped to design the framework for the publication: Sr. Brenda Cherry, OSP, Principal, St. Benedict the Moor School (Washington, DC); Ms. Wilma Durham, Principal, Archbishop Carroll High School, (Washington, DC); Ms. Therese Wilson Favors, Director of African-American Catholic Ministry, Archdiocese of Baltimore; Mr. Kirk Gaddy, Assistant Principal, St. Katharine's School (Baltimore); Sr. Barbara Spears, SNJM, Principal, St. Gabriel's School (Washington, DC); Ms. Edith Stevens, Teacher, St. Therese of the Child Jesus School (Philadelphia); and Ms. Jacqueline Wilson, Director, Office of Black Catholics, Archdiocese of Washington.

Gratitude is also due to Rev. Clarence R. J. Rivers of Stimuli Inc. in Cincinnati, for numerous consultations about the book including the suggestion of the title and rationale behind it as well as contributing the artwork for the publication. Many thanks to Ms. Donna Ashaka, a staff member with the Secretariat for African-American Catholics, for her research work on the "Model Schools" chapter. And finally, thanks to Ms. Maxine Rivers, who coordinated the project, and to members of the NCEA staff who assisted most ably in getting this book into print: Ms. Patricia Feistritzer, Ms. Tia Gray, Mr. Michael Guerra, Ms. Phyllis Kokus, Ms. Tara McCallum, Ms. Beatriz Ruiz and Ms. Leah Cosumano (an NCEA intern from Georgetown University).

Funding for the development of this manuscript came from the Fr. Michael J. McGivney Fund for New Initiatives in Catholic Education, sponsored by the Knights of Columbus.

"**I**t is still my joy to remember that St. George's Church and School provided me the inspiration and motivation to rise above the sense of hopelessness that characterizes so many who grow up in poverty. It is my joy that what I gained there has sustained me throughout my life."

Most Rev. James P. Lyke
Archbishop of Atlanta
from his address to the
National Congress on Catholic Schools
for the 21st Century, 1990

"Can These Bones Live?"

An Overview of African-American Catholic Culture and History

Dr. Giles A. Conwill

African-American Catholics share three cultural systems: the African, the American and the Catholic. *Culture* may be defined as

> ... the vast structures of behaviors, ideas, attitudes, values, habits, beliefs, customs, language, rituals, ceremonies and practices peculiar to a particular group of people which provide them with a general design for living and patterns for interpreting reality.[1]

Because they are a part of the "African diaspora"—i.e., people of African descent who are dispersed around the world—they share in the fundamental matrix of culture(s) of Africa.

As "Africans in America," African Americans have assimilated many "American" values, yet they have developed a distinct culture: one of resistance and survivability as they have lived in this land through slavery, Jim Crow segregation, the Civil Rights era, the Black Consciousness and Black Power movements, and the present period of Black Political Empowerment.

African-American Catholics also share the general cultural rubric that is Catholicism. Catholic theologian Patrick Granfield in his *Ecclesial Cybernetics* reminds us how powerful this Catholic "cultural" system is at molding ideas, customs, behaviors and rituals as it employs both its teaching authority *(magisterium)* and tradition to fulfill its mission to proclaim the Gospel *(Kerygma),* form communi-

ty *(Koinonia)* and serve the world *(Diakonia)*. This former professor of The Catholic University of America describes the Catholic Church as

> ...an assembly, the eschatologically redeemed community that professes the Lordship of Jesus Christ, that ratifies its faith by sacramental baptism, and that is joined together by a threefold unity: a unity of *creed* (an affirmation of essential doctrines); a unity of *code* (an acknowledgement of common moral precepts as well as papal and collegial authority); and a unity of *cult* (a participation in a sevenfold sacramental system).[2]

African-American Catholics are beginning to appreciate how so many of the customs and rituals of Judaism and Christianity are rooted in the magnificent African religion of ancient Egypt.

African-American Catholics are becoming more aware and proud of their history and culture. They are beginning to celebrate Afrocentricity and the richness of their African heritage as they are brought to light and shared through the scholarly works of the late Cheikh Anta Diop Molefi Asante, Maulana Karenga, Asa Hilliard and others. They are beginning to see that their history and heritage are rooted in a time and place before the transatlantic European slave trade, wherein strong family and kinship bonds and a sense of collective responsibility were norms. They are beginning to appreciate how so many of the customs and rituals of Judaism and Christianity are rooted in the magnificent African religion of ancient Egypt *(Kemet)*. Black Catholics, aided by a small cadre of Black Catholic scholars, are also learning their story as it has unfolded in North America. The purpose of this chapter will be to investigate the African roots of the faith and culture of African-American Catholics and show how it has unfolded in their history.

Christ and Africa. The two encountered each other long ago, and thus began the syncretic connection between Christian faith and African culture which so vigorously survives even to this day in various forms throughout the world. Both history and Sacred Scripture testify that Africa and her children played a significant role not only in the Old Testament[3] but also in the life of Jesus of Nazareth, and the religion which he established.

For example, legend has it that one of the three Magi who visited the Christ Child was black. These three "wise men," coming from different parts of the world, were a symbol of the Gentiles becoming Christian. Reportedly coming from Africa, Asia and Europe, they were "ambassadors" representing the entire world at the Epiphany. Since Africa was at that time considered to be one of the "ends of the earth," the Black king represented in his own person the evangelistic nature which characterizes Christianity's missionary spirit and global outreach program.

Africa is strategically present at the beginning and at the end of the life of Jesus. It was Africa that provided safe refuge for the infant when Herod sought to murder him along with the other "Innocents," for Joseph was commanded to take the child and his mother to Egypt.(Matt 2:13) They remained there until Herod died. An African,

Simon of Cyrene, helped the "man of sorrows" bear the cross on his way to Calvary Hill.

The African connection did not stop here. The New Testament story of the Ethiopian treasurer of the Queen of Ethiopia (Meroe) in Acts 8 presents an intelligent, literate, responsible black man who was trying to understand what was written in the scroll containing the writings of the prophet Isaiah. He is very significant in the story of Christianity because when Philip baptized him, this black man became the first biblical example of a non-Jew to be baptized. Thus he may be considered the "prototypical Gentile." Africans, as shown by the story of the Magi and the Ethiopian eunuch, are symbols of the extent to which Christianity is enjoined to reach out to all persons, even to the ends of the earth.

The divine imperative *"Euntes, docete omnes gentes!"* ("While going, teach all nations!") makes it clear that Christianity is to be an aggressively vigorous and proselytizing religion. Jesus intended for the movement that he founded to be thenceforth open to all persons, all places, all times. This intentionality of universalism may even be seen in Jesus' birthplace. He was born in the Middle East, the crossroads of the then-known world. It was indeed, literally "Medi-terranean," i.e., at the "center of the world." The bearers of the Good News would take advantage of this historical setting and cultural ambience and thus be spirited along on cultural highways already established by the extensive Roman Empire to reach the *oikoimene,* all the known world.

The "race" of the Messiah also carried symbolic overtones of a worldwide mission to all mankind. As anthropologist Ali Mazrui states, Jesus could not have chosen a more appropriate people among whom to be born than the "Semitic sector of mankind" because they represent such an amalgam of humanity:

> There is a profound racial ambiguity about the Jews and there is a profound pigmentational ambiguity among Arabs. Arabs as a "race" are impossible to classify by pigmentation. The range of colors of these people is from the white Arabs of Lebanon and Syria, the brown Arabs of the Hadhramout, to the black Arabs of the Sudan and parts of Saudi Arabia.[4]

This very ambiguity, because it defies strict racial classification, implies a diffusion, multiple allegiances and the possibility of numerous affiliations. This Messiah is not just for the Jews. In John 12:32, we hear Jesus saying, "And when I am lifted from the earth, I shall draw all men to myself." The man from Galilee was indeed to become the "desire of all nations."

Another source of pride for people of the African diaspora is that Africa could boast of flourishing Christian communities long before Europe's conversion. Christianity was thriving in North Africa as early as the fourth century.[5] Ireland, on the other hand, was not converted until St. Patrick's arrival in the fifth century. Anglo-Saxons had to wait for St. Gregory in the sixth. Evangelization efforts in northern Germany were initiated in the eighth century by St. Boniface. Even Poland, which is so heavily Catholic today, was not converted to Christianity until the year 1000.

I consider Africa a co-cradle of Christianity because the faith was nurtured there in its early days. As mentioned above, it was particularly strong in Alexandria, Carthage and Ethiopia. From practically the beginning Africa's contribution to the Judaeo-Christian faith included martyrs, defenders of the faith and even popes.

Saints Perpetua and Felicity were martyred in 203 A.D. in Carthage for their staunch allegiance to Christianity.[6] Tertullian, Origen and St. Cyprian, Africans all, were early Christian theologians. St. Augustine (b. 354), a native of Numidia, North Africa, was a "Doctor of the Church" and is perhaps most famous for *Confessions, City of God* and his hundreds of homilies which helped formulate many tenets of Christian theology. St. Athanasius (b. 297), patriarch of his birthplace Alexandria, Egypt, earned the title "Champion of Orthodoxy" for his defense of the divinity of Christ and his condemnation of Arianism. He was present at the deliberations of the Council of Nicea in 325.

There have been three African popes: St. Victor I (189-199), St. Melchiades (311-314) and St. Gelasius I (492-496). Although their reigns were short, they accomplished amazingly much. Victor I settled a major dispute by ordering that the celebration of Easter be on the Sunday following the 14th day of the vernal equinox. Melchiades was pope when Constantine promulgated the Edict of Milan (313), which allowed for freedom of worship for Christianity. When Constantine's wife presented him with the Lateran Palace in Rome, Melchiades became the first pope to have an official residence.[7]

Pope St. Gelasius' greatest contribution is perhaps in the area of liturgical worship. The composition of the Gelasian Sacramentary, which later gave birth to the Roman Rite, is attributed to him. He also settled a dispute by allowing the Eucharist to be administered with or without wine and established the feast of the Purification (Candlemas). Regarding the question of whether or not these African popes were *Black* Africans is still open to debate.[8] Nevertheless, they still are a source of pride for African Americans.

Butler's *Lives of the Saints,* the most complete listing of saints in the English language, indicates that there were many early monks and hermits living in the deserts of North Africa around this time. The seeds and roots of early Christian monasticism began in North Africa.

Egypt and nearly all of North Africa remained Christian until c. 640 A.D. as part of the Byzantine Empire. Muslim Arabs began their conquest of Egypt in that year, and by 698 Islamic tribes had taken the entire North African coast. Ethiopia, however, did not fall prey to them and remained a Christian bastion.[9] It is notable that when the Portuguese began their incursions into Africa in search of servile labor, they would use the excuse that they were merely reinstating Christianity where it had been up to the seventh century. To its credit, another Christian bastion, Nubia, located in the upper Egypt-Sudan area, tenaciously survived until the 1280s and 1290s when attacks from Moslem Egypt succeeded in destroying its Christian foundations also.

Sub-Saharan Africa remained virtually untouched by Christianity up to the inception of the slave trade. In that region of the continent, tribes generally practiced traditional African religions. Although traditional African religions are numerous, they all have certain characteristics in common: 1) belief in one supreme God; 2) belief that God is both immanent and transcendent; 3) ancestor worship; 4) a sense of responsibility for the welfare of the whole group; 5) a profound respect for nature; and 6) belief that death is not the end of life, but merely a stage in it.[10]

Islam was the other major form of religion practiced in sub-Saharan Africa. The "pillars of this faith," which were introduced in the seventh century, are 1) the creed— "There is no God but Allah, and Muhammad is his messenger"; 2) prayer

five times daily; 3) almsgiving; 4) fasting from sunup to sundown during the month of Ramadan (the month that the Angel Gabriel was to have relayed the Koran to Muhammad on behalf of Allah); and 5) the *hajj* or pilgrimage to Mecca at least once in a lifetime.

Islam made a tremendous impact on West Africa. Many kings adopted Islam, as did their subjects. One king, Mansa Musa, from the Empire of Mali in the 14th century, made a pilgrimage across Africa through Egypt to Mecca that was of such impact that it was even recorded in the annals of Europe. His huge caravan included 100 camelloads of gold, which, when he generously spread them around in Cairo, destabilized that city's economy for some years to come.[11]

As mentioned above, sub-Saharan Africa remained virtually untouched by Christianity until the inception of the slave trade. When the Church did involve herself there, her history was a checkered one indeed, checkered because she played the roles of both proponent and opponent of slavery. For example, Popes Nicholas V (1454) and Calixtus III (1456) promulgated official documents that encouraged Portugal to enslave sub-Saharan Africans so that they could be converted.[12] On the other hand, no fewer than five popes condemned the slave trade: Pius II on October 7, 1462; Paul III on May 29, 1537; Urban VIII on April 2, 1639; Benedict XIV on December 20, 1741; and Gregory XVI on December 3, 1839.[13] Obviously, papal condemnations had little effect.

Perhaps the most famous (or infamous) individual Church figure responsible for encouraging a policy of African enslavement was the Spanish Bishop Bartolome de Las Casas. Living up to his title "Protector of the Indians," he suggested the importation of Blacks into Hispaniola (1517) because the indigenous people (Indians) were dying of overwork.[14] His suggestion was heeded and his observations about the frailty of the Indians and the strength of the Africans were likewise shared by King Ferdinand of Spain, for the Spanish monarch wrote that "one Black could do the work of four Indians."[15] De Las Casas later repented, reversed his position and became a strong advocate of anti-slavery to such an extent that he refused absolution to slave owners. The vehement opposition then marshalled against the Dominican prelate resulted in his being hounded by his See and returning to Spain.

Spain was one of several countries which, at one time or another, held the coveted *asiento*—the formal contract between the papal office, crowns and companies, that granted the "privilege" of bartering in Black flesh in certain sections of Africa and the New World. Other countries included France, England, Holland and Portugal, the first major transporter of Blacks. The popes signed the *asiento* and received a fee. They were also arbiters when disputes arose among nations.

The following indicates the periods during which these countries engaged in the slave trade.[16]

	Beginning of Slave Trade	**Official/Unofficial End of Slavery**
Portugal	1444	1853/1870
Spain	1479	1835
England	1562	1807
U.S.	1619	1808/1861
Holland	1625	1795/1803
France	1642	1833/1860
Sweden	1647	1825
Denmark	1697	1792

We shall never know how many Africans were stolen from their homelands and forced into lifelong servitude. We shall never know how many died along the "Middle Passage" on the ships, nor how many bleached bones lie at the bottom of the Atlantic, nor how many were eaten by the swarms of hungry sharks that reportedly followed slave ships. The estimate of the number of Africans taken from Africa—based on extant slave cargo inventory records and ships' logs and from demographic studies/agricultural productivity technology—ranges from a high of 50 million (by scholars such as W.E.B. DuBois and Basil Davidson) to a low of 11.5 million by Philip Curtin in his *Atlantic Slave Trade: A Census*.[17] Curtin maintained that only 9.5 million actually reached the New World. Scholars have argued that these figures are too low.

Most of the Africans brought to the New World came from West Africa, and this transatlantic phase of the European slave trade dispersed Africans throughout the New World (North, Central, and South America). A relatively small number of East Africans were brought over, for they were part of the Arab/Muslim slave trade in East Africa which basically supplied the Indian Ocean slave trade.[18]

These Africans brought their culture along with them on their sea journey. The influential early scholarship of anthropologist Melville Herskovits' *The Myth of the Negro Past*[19] regarding African cultural retentions present in Blacks in North America has been expanded by others. These so-called "Africanisms" may be found in language, music, religion, behavior, diet and a host of other factors which comprise and affect culture. Let us look at some of these.

LANGUAGE

West Africans who were brought to the Americas spoke many diverse tribal languages and dialects, but in this slaving group there were two main language groups: Bantu and the Sudanic.[20] West African language patterns and syntactical and grammatical elements can be seen in the languages spoken by Blacks in the New World. Ethnolinguist J.L. Dillard makes this point very straightforwardly:

> Today there is a clear-cut case of a variety of American English, related to West African varieties in Gullah, which is spoken on the Sea Islands off Georgia and South Carolina. French Creole, mutually intelligible with Haitian French Creole, is spoken in Louisiana and southeastern Texas. Both of these languages are related to the Caribbean Creoles. Recent research presents evidence that the English of most American Blacks retains some features which are common to both Caribbean and West African varieties of English....American Black English can be traced to a creolized version of English based upon a pidgin spoken by slaves.[21]

Asante describes the process of pidginization and creolization:

> According to creolization theory, a pidgin language is characterized by two factors: its grammatical system is sharply reduced, and it is not the native language system of those who speak it. When pidgin becomes the native language of those who use it, it becomes a Creole language.[22]

As Africans struggled to learn English, they approximated some of the sounds in English that were not in their languages to those that were close to sounds in their own phonetic repertoire. For example, the "th" sound in "this" and "that" became "dis" and "tat." Another characteristic is the "durative be." In many languages the

verb "to be" is superfluous—not really needed to convey the meaning. So-called Black English, sometimes referred to as Ebonics or Afrish (compare to Spanish and English), may be non-Standard English, but it too follows certain rules, as may be seen in these examples of the durative "be": "He be going" (instead of "he is going"). Notice the following examples of Black English show the sense of tense clearly: "he gone," "he been gone," "he done been gone." Many African Americans practice bilingualism: They are conversant in Standard English and their own regional race-specific idiom. Sometimes these idioms manifest the trait of double entendre (use of double meanings) that may be seen in the spirituals and the blues, wherein a reserved meaning for one's in-group accompanies the overt one.

MUSIC

Music is another important example of how African Americans as a people of the African diaspora share the cultural matrix of the motherland. Ethnomusicologist Portia Maultsby provides a very useful historical schema for the development of African-American music and the West African roots for such music. Among the musical forms she lists are spirituals, blues, gospel, work songs, game songs, boogie-woogie, rhythm and blues, rock and roll, civil rights songs, ragtime, jazz, swing bands, bebop, soul, go-go, disco, funk and rap.[23]

According to John Lovell, the African-American Spirituals numerically represent the greatest contribution to American folk songs:

> The Americanized Scottish ballad, the patriotic song, the sea and river songs, the comic and nonsense song, the nursery and children's song, the play-party song, the courtship song, the dance song, the historical song, the crime song, the jailbird song, the railroad ballad, the hobo and bum song, the street song, the mountain song, the mining song, the temperance song, the cowboy and cattle song, the lumberman's song, and the songs of countries from which Americans come—any one group is small by comparison with the American slave song.[24]

RELIGION

The religions practiced by Africans in the African diaspora in the New World also manifest West African roots. Albert Raboteau, Orlando Patterson, Roger Bastide, Henry Mitchell, Joseph Washington, Erskine Clarke and Margaret Washington Creel are but a few of the fine scholars who have engaged in the study of this phenomenon.

We have already seen that West Africans were practicing traditional African religions and Islam. When they were brought to the New World, their exposure to Christianity was not the same for all. The colonizer who enslaved him/her and the colony to which he/she was brought determined, in large measure, the slave's treatment and the evangelistic efforts expended on his/her behalf. For instance, the Catholic French, Spanish and Portuguese felt more responsible for the evangelization of their slaves—having come in the names of both Crown and Cross—than did the British. Differences in political systems, and Roman vs. Anglo-Saxon law, affected the manner of treatment. Frank Tannenbaum observes:

> Those who were enslaved in the Spanish and Portuguese colonies entered a culture that was Catholic in religion, semi-medieval and authoritarian in its political institutions, conservative and paternalistic in its social relations, and Roman in its system of law. Africans brought to America, by contrast, confronted a culture that

was Protestant in religion, libertarian and "modern" in its political institutions, individualistic in its social relations, and Anglo-Saxon in its system of laws.[25]

The French *Code Noire* of 1685 and the Spanish Slave Code of 1789 (which incorporated ideas from the former) proclaimed that "slaves must be given education in religious matters; the master must provide this."[26] The British did not concern themselves with conversion of Africans until late into the 18th century.

The colony to which the slave was brought determined not only the denomination of Christianity (Catholic, Baptist, Methodist, Quaker, etc.) to which he would be exposed, and the quality and mode of evangelization, but also the formal aspects of the worship act—including the "god" to whom homage was given. Albert Raboteau makes an insightful distinction between the Africans who were brought to the Caribbean and South America, and those who were brought to what is now continental United States. Those Africans who were brought to the Caribbean and South America retained not only their African rituals and styles of worship but also their African gods. Rituals and cults of these transplanted African gods include Candomble in Brazil, Shango in Trinidad and vodun or voodoo in Haiti. The African gods here are said to be "in exile." These gods are syncretized and "meshed in" with Christian ritual.

Raboteau characterizes the religion of those Africans who were brought to the mainland United States differently. Here, the African gods no longer live. They have been supplanted by the Christian God. African gods may be gone but African *styles* of worship remain. Stylistic elements include rhythmic hand clapping, foot tapping, pulpit oratory, singing, and pew talk which exhibits call-and-response. Even the way black choirs sway back and forth harkens back to African religious dancing which hypnotically readies one for the descent and "possession" by the spirit of the gods.[27]

Today most African-American Christians are affiliated with the Baptist and Methodist traditions, primarily because these denominations were the major ones in the South during the era of slavery. Before 1740 the African Americans' religious worship system was mainly characterized by their "primitive" beliefs. From 1740-1790 the "Great Awakening" spurred active overtures of evangelization on the part of the Protestant denominations, particularly Baptists, Methodists and Presbyterians. Black Baptist churches began to appear as early as the Revolutionary War era with the Silver Bluff Church in Savannah, Georgia (1773-75). The African Methodist Episcopal Church has its roots in the 1787 establishment of the Free African Society, when a disgruntled Richard Allen left the discrimination experienced in a Methodist church to form an African denomination.

All of the Christian denominations to some degree acquiesced to the racist policies which have prevailed throughout the various periods of this country's history. Catholic leaders and laity could be found on both sides of the issue: some opposed slavery and racism and sought emancipation for Blacks, while others favored the status quo.

Catholicism in Colonial America was a struggling sectlike foundation with few adequate resources to devote even to its white adherents. The Jesuits and Sulpicians who introduced Catholicism to Colonial America, along with the missionaries who later accompanied immigrants, found their resources and manpower nearly exhausted with the work at hand. Slavery, in general, was perceived by the American Catholic Church as a political issue and an institution of the State. The Church was not to interfere in matters political; therefore she saw her responsibility restricted to

that of ensuring the religious education and formation of those in bondage. Some ecclesiastics even emphasized the positive effect of slavery by picturing it as a missionary institution: It facilitated the Christianizing of these captive pagans from Africa.

Catholics were ambivalent in policy and practice. For example, in antebellum New Orleans, with its sizeable number of free Blacks, when other churches were rigidly segregated, "free Negroes owned half of the pews in St. Augustine's Catholic Church and attended many other Catholic churches in New Orleans without having any distinction made against them."[28] Louisiana, however, was a Southern exception. Before special parishes were provided for blacks, the general seating pattern for them seems to have been unsegregated seating in the North, while in the South Blacks were generally relegated to sections designated as "the colored pews."

During the Civil War era, the issue of slavery divided Catholics along sectional lines in the same way it did the rest of the nation's population. Northern Catholics were generally in sympathy with the Union, while their Southern counterparts tended to support the Confederacy and its aims. When the major Protestant denominations split in the mid-1840s into Northern and Southern branches over the issue of slavery (e.g., "Southern" Baptists) or the attempt of the "United" Methodist Church to later mend the breech in Methodism, Catholics did not split.[29] However, while there was no official denominational split between Northern and Southern Catholics, there was a brief attempt to gain Vatican acknowledgement of the sovereignty of the Confederacy when the Confederate government sent Bishop Patrick Lynch of Charleston in 1864 as its ambassadorial representative, but Rome accepted him merely in the capacity of an ordinary bishop.[30] While Catholic bishops tried to maintain a stance of political neutrality regarding the Civil War, Catholic officers and soldiers fought in both Union and Confederate armies. Catholic priests served as chaplains for both sides: over 40 for the Union and nearly 30 for the Confederate troops.

▲
▼

The Catholic Church, realizing that 100,000 of the four million emancipated blacks were Catholics, felt a renewed sense of responsibility for their evangelization.

▲
▼

During the Reconstruction era after the war, the Catholic Church, realizing that 100,000 of the four million emancipated blacks were Catholics, felt a renewed sense of responsibility for their evangelization. Various bishops around the country, particularly those in the poverty-stricken and devastated South, were faced with the moral and ethical duty to do something for the newly freed black sheep of their respective flocks. Southern dioceses had little wealth and few personnel. The ravages of war had simply made things worse. One can easily imagine the frustration, for example, of Bishop Lynch of Charleston, who reported that 20,000 of the 750,000 emancipated blacks in South Carolina were Catholics.[31]

The bishops acknowledged that this was a national problem which required a collective-and-national-level solution. So, in 1866, 45 bishops from around the country

convened in Baltimore the Second Plenary Council. This was the first of several meetings on the national and local levels which addressed black Catholic evangelization. The episcopal leaders requested that a search be undertaken throughout dioceses of this country and Europe for priests and sisters who would devote themselves to the black apostolate. They sought the establishment of some American society or congregation of clergy and nuns for ministry to blacks. They agreed to petition the pope to canonize Benedict the Moor and Martin de Porres so that blacks would have their own saintly models. They requested that Peter Claver be declared not only a saint but also principal "Patron of the Negroes." The bishops directed that efforts of evangelization be extended toward blacks both within and outside the Catholic faith. Missions exclusively dedicated to their care were encouraged. Schools and orphanages were built, and positive programs on regional levels were implemented.

A bit later, the Third Plenary Council of Baltimore instituted an annual "Negro and Indian Missions Collection" which was to be taken up throughout the country to support the evangelization of these peoples. It continues to this day.

One of the more effective proposals was the bishops' decree that an all-out effort be initiated to instruct black converts and, in those areas where it was deemed necessary, to have separate and special parishes for them. These parishes were not to be confused with or placed in the same category as the independent Black Protestant churches; nor was forced segregation the motive behind their establishment.[32] They were simply to be places where a specialized apostolate devoted to Black proselytization and ministry would take place. Black Catholics were to remain part of the same denomination and subject to the same jurisdictions of the respective dioceses in which they lived.

The history of Black-American Catholicism represents a rich tapestry of faith. It includes the story of the founding of the three orders of Black women religious: in Baltimore, the Oblate Sisters of Providence (1829); in New Orleans, the Sisters of the Holy Family (1842) (note that both of these were founded before the Emancipation Proclamation of 1863); and in Savannah, Georgia, the Franciscan Handmaids of the Most Pure Heart of Mary (1917), presently headquartered in Harlem, New York. The history includes the story of the first African-American priests, the Healy brothers, Augustus Tolton, Charles Uncles, and a small army of others. It includes Katharine Drexel, Xavier University, the Sisters of the Blessed Sacrament, the Josephites and the Society of the Divine Word.

The religious saga of African-American evangelization reveals dedicated and saintly lay persons, too, such as Pierre Toussaint, Daniel Rudd, Thomas Wyatt Turner, Mathilda Beasley, Dr. Lena Edwards, Jackie Wilson, Maye Turner and the Knights and Ladies Auxiliary of St. Peter Claver. It encompasses the workings of the Holy Spirit as it directed the founding of the National Office for Black Catholics, the Black Clergy Conference and Sisters' Caucus, the Black Secretariat, the many diocesan offices of Black Catholic ministry around the country, and the National Black Catholic Congresses of the last and the present centuries.

The history of Black American Catholicism includes and has been enriched by passionate preachers like Jim Goode and George Stallings; musicians like Rawn Harbor, Grayson Brown and Leon Roberts; visionaries like Joseph Davis, Joseph Slattery and Archbishop James Lyke; shepherd-hearted pastors like Bill Norvell, Teresita Wind and Michael Pfleger; stalwart pioneers like Clarence Rivers and Walter Hubbard; gifted black thinkers such as Shawn Copeland, Bede Abrams and Joseph

Nieron; calls for a new rite; the non-closure of Catholic schools; and chroniclers of it all, like Cyprian Davis and myself.

The prophetic call of African-American Catholics challenges the Church to undertake liturgical adaptation that takes black culture seriously, to engage in preaching and ministry that give perspective and impetus to black Catholic empowerment, and to redress the racism, tokenism and lack of affirmative action in the Church, especially as shown by the failure to promote more black bishops who are really in touch with their people's needs. The church should also address the need for seminary faculty and students to become more sensitive to and informed about black culture and history; for vocational literature and programs that reflect black and other so-called "minority" groups; and for religious education resources with black and multiethnic awareness. Finally, the church should respond to the call for serious training of white ministers working in black parishes, along with a progressive dealing with the problems of black lay leadership development in a white, clergy-dominated, hierarchically structured Church.

Yes, African-American Catholics with their culture and history throw down the gauntlet of prophetic challenge to the Church in the same way that Black Americans have presented a challenge to this nation. The United States claims to hold certain truths to be inalienable; Black Americans have been America's conscience, goading it to live up to that claim. Similarly, African-American Catholics challenge their Church to live up to its claims of "catholicity" so that they and other "others" may feel at home in this eschatologically redeemed community which is united in the threefold unity of creed, cult and code, and which—most importantly—professes the Lordship of Jesus Christ.

NOTES

1. Nobles cited in Asa Hilliard and Lucretia Payton-Stewart and Larry O. Williams, *Infusion of African and African American Content in the School Curriculum: The Proceedings of the First National Conference,* Morristown, NJ, Aaron Press, 1989, p. 6.

2. Patrick Granfield, *Ecclesial Cybernetics: A Systems Analysis of Authority and Decision-Making in the Catholic Church, With A Plea for Shared Responsibility,* New York, The Macmillan Company, 1973, p. 8.

3. Cain Hope Felder, *Troubling Biblical Waters: Race, Class, and Family,* Mary Knoll, NY, Orbis Books, 1989.

4. Ali A. Mazrui, *The African Condition,* New York, Cambridge University Press, 1980, p. 13.

5. Noel Erskine, *Decolonizing Theology: A Caribbean Perspective,* Mary Knoll, NY, Orbis Books, 1981, p. 33.

6. Robert Fulton Holtzclaw, *The Saints Go Marching In,* Shaker Heights, OH, The Keeble Press, 1980, p. 130.

7. Ibid., pp. 112-114.

8. Cyprian Davis, *The History of Black Catholics in the United States,* New York, The Crossroad Publishing Company, 1990, p. 13.

9. Paul Bohanon and Philip Curtin, *Africa and Africans,* Garden City, NY, The National History Press, 1971, p. 253.

10. Karenga cited in Gayraud S. Wilmore, *African American Religious Studies: An Interdisciplinary Anthology,* Durham, NC, Duke University Press, 1989, p. 272.

11. Kevin Shillington, *History of Africa,* London, The Macmillan Company, 1989, p. 98.

12. Leslie B. Rout, *The African Experience in Spanish America: 1502 to the Present Day,* New York, Cambridge University Press, 1976, p. 11.

13. Frank Tannenbaum, *Slave and Citizen,* New York, Vintage Books, 1963, p. 62.

14. Rout, op. cit., p. 23.

15. Ibid.

16. Molefi Asante and Mark Mattson, *Historical and Cultural Atlas of African Americans,* New York, Macmillan Publishing Company, 1992.

17. Philip Curtin, *The Atlantic Slave Trade: A Census,* Madison, The University of Wisconsin Press, 1969.

18. Tariq Azevedo, ed., *African Studies: A Survey of Africa and the African Diaspora,* Durham, NC, Carolina Academic Press, 1993, p. 75.

19. Melville Herskovits, *The Myth of the Negro Past,* Boston, Beacon Press, 1958.

20. Ibid., pp. 77-81.

21. Joey Lee Dillard, *Black English: Its History and Usage in the United States,* New York, Vintage Books, 1972, p. 6.

22. Asante cited in Joseph Holloway, *Africanisms in American Culture,* Bloomington, Indiana University Press, 1990, p. 22.

23. Maultsby, cited in Holloway, p. 186.

24. John Lovell, *Black Song: The Forge and the Flame,* New York, The Macmillan Company, 1972, p. 220.

25. Tannenbaum cited in Gary Nash, *Red, White, and Black: The Peoples of Early America,* Englewood Cliffs, NJ, Prentice Hall Inc., 1974, p. 173.

26. Rout, op. cit., pp. 84-85.

27. Albert Raboteau, *Slave Religion: The "Invisible Institution" in the Antebellum South,* New York, Oxford University Press, 1978.

28. John W. Blassingame, *Black New Orleans 1860-1880,* Chicago, The University of Chicago Press, 1973, p. 16.

29. John Tracy Ellis, *American Catholicism,* Chicago, The University of Chicago Press, 1956, p. 91.

30. Ibid., p. 95.

31. Ibid., p. 99.

32. Joseph Leonard, *Theology and Race Relations,* Milwaukee, The Bruce Publishing Company, 1963, p. 229.

"**To bear good fruit, catechesis must be rooted in the spirituality of the people and couched in the language they best understand.**"

Sr. Thea Bowman
Educator, Writer, Consultant
In *Shooting Star:*
Selected Writings and Speeches

"We All Got a Right to the Tree of Life"

Transforming the Curriculum for Inclusion

Sr. Eva Regina Martin, SSF

There is a voice present in every culture.

As differing cultural groups pursue differing ways of life, it stands to reason that each would have its own particular way of perceiving, creating, appreciating, defining, and understanding, yet, at the same time responding to other cultures as being just as beautiful, just as holistic as their own; no better, no less.

All of us are one, and one of us is all...

Silence from and about the subject was the order of the day. Some of the silences were broken, and some are maintained by authors who lived with and within the policing strategies. What I am interested in are the strategies for breaking it.[1]

Toni Morrison

Freedom is not something given: it is something you conquer—collectively.[2]

Stephen May

THE DEBATE OVER THE CANON: POLITICAL AND HISTORICAL CORRECTNESS

There are new and innovative methods to be used in the teaching of children. But first, we must employ the process of what has been called "political correctness." Within this open dialogue, issues will be presented so as to engage a response from you, the reader, to appreciate the challenge placed before you as an educator. It is hoped that a constructive approach will lend itself to the debate over multiculturalism and its implications for all cultures, because it is the holistic approach to the

teaching of all children. It is good to be aware of debates on multiculturalism's use as an educational tool, for these debates direct the issue toward concerns educators may have not considered. It is far more advantageous, however, to dwell on multiculturalism's implications for the curriculum, because it is the curriculum which will transform the mindset of children.

Paul Berman, in what will soon become a classic, has opened the debate on political correctness by publishing a text titled *Debating P.C.: The Controversy over Political Correctness on College Campuses.* This book has pooled ideas from prominent scholars in order to bring to the American table the debate on the issue over preparing Americans for a wider world (inclusive, liberal) or narrowing academic freedom (exclusive, conservative). Terms such as "hegemonic" and "non-hegemonic" have enabled these scholars to frame opposing views within the debate on political correctness. The debate grew out of Stanford University's decision to abolish the Western curriculum for a more plausible multicultural curriculum through "emphasizing the work and history made by women, by persons of color, and by natives of the Third World."[3]

The debt that Western civilization owes to the Native-American, Asian and African cultures has to be acknowledged and corrected in the theology, history and geography books in classrooms.

The exchanges and views within the debate are unsettling but informative. The debate is a long overdue concern about education within a pluralistic society. Like all new data that have been placed within the educational arena, this debate focuses on who controls knowledge. This controversy has, in part, evoked a decisive debate over what scholars believe constitutes an American identity.

In defending the present curriculum, Dinnish D'Souza and his colleagues, who are the critics of multiculturalism, have asserted a conservative, Western traditionalist view of education (writers who want to center only the Western canon within the curriculum). These scholars propose the idea that education should be about equality of opportunity, about giving everyone a fair chance. Education should not be about racial preference. Education should have high standards instead of attacking academia as being primarily a white male-dominated society.[4] Stimpson, Howe, Cramer and Kimball state that multiculturalism will debunk the present curriculum of "classics of Western civilization to replace parts of the curriculum with women's issues and cultural issues which will weaken the curriculum."[5] The agenda for the Western canon theorizes that divisiveness is the only possible outcome of any alternatives.

Schools are powerful institutions. Schools are sources of learning, socialization and indoctrination. (Children learn socialization skills from educators preparing them to live in a multicultural society.) Schools can also dispel myths and/or perpetuate them. However, the labeling of America as a multicultural society represents a contradiction. We are all implicated in this misrepresentation by the positions we hold about society, culture and education. In regard to a pluralistic society, the cur-

rent curriculum does not address the souls of its students. What the traditionalists do not realize is that multiculturalism is in conformity with the democratic ideals of life.

This debate and the responses to it have been centered around the views of many scholars rather than the community of American individuals within the learning environment. Individuals learn their community cultures at an early age. However, when they enter a learning environment, their cultures are displaced so that the hegemonic culture may be known. The scholarship of "multiculturalism" would help to initiate a new thrust for other cultures to view their own history. For many scholars, such as Said and his colleagues Searless, West, Gates, and Pollitt, the present system is another form of imperialism that has failed and impoverished the souls of today's students.[6] Scholars who are interested in creating a new paradigm for today's students should read authors such as Said, Banks, Morrison, Minnich, Banal and West.

The above thinkers are of the opinion that, since we are a unique society, the present curriculum is killing the spirit and energy of the American way of life. Edward Said comments:

> The history of "Western civilization" is, for the most part, a history of oppression. Internally, Western civilization oppressed women, various slave and serf populations, and ethnic/cultural minorities generally. In foreign affairs, the history of Western civilization is one of imperialism and colonialism. One cannot reform the present system because "the canon" has to be abolished. It has to be abolished in favor of something that is "multicultural" and "non-hierarchical."[7]

Artist Rick Hill further illustrates the effect of Western oppression by saying:

> When I'm at home I'm one kind of person, when I'm on the reservation, I'm another, when I go out in public I'm another, when I'm the only Indian in the crowd I'm still another, so it's like I'm a multifaceted person who reflects this situation so that they are all equally important, but that's the way Indians are dealing with the white man or mainstream culture. We're constantly confronted with things non-Indian, and therefore to me it's only logical—and this is what bothers me about Indian art—that we should address the things that impact on our lives, instead of pretending that all Indians are in this spiritual nirvana somewhere. We have to deal with the reality...that not all Indians like being Indians, and that there is still a battle on for hearts and minds. I...see my art as a defensive mechanism to create some sort of visual legacy that will turn Indians on to wanting to remain Indian and see that we have the power of thinking.[8]

Concepts that are congruous to this perspective are non-hegemonic, non-patriarchal or non-exclusionary. This approach acknowledges ethnic, racial and religious voice distinctions and provides avenues for challenging stereotypes placed on groups of people.

The position usually taken by traditionalists is being threatened by corrective history, the inclusion of other cultures and the voices of women and people of color. Other cultures, and women also, want their history within the curriculum. The debt that Western civilization owes to the Native-American, Asian and African cultures has to be acknowledged and corrected in the theology, history and geography books and in classrooms. The language in which cultures have been described also has to be corrected. For example, the use of the word "primitive" in describing ancient people is negative in scope and framing. The European culture has not been described as

primitive, so why should there be anything primitive about African, Asian and Native-American cultures? At faculty meetings, teachers can come together and delete pernicious words such as "primitive," "tribes" or "minority" that place negative connotations on cultures.

In discussing multicultural education, James Banks makes a thoughtful and engaging analysis when he states:

> We should teach students that knowledge is a social construction, that it reflects the perspectives, experiences, and the values of the people and the cultures that construct it, and is debated among knowledge creators.... The fact that multi-culturalists want to reformulate and transform the Western canon, not purge the curriculum of the West, is absent from most of the writings of the Western traditionalists.[9]

What multiculturalists are trying to frame is a system whereby all Americans feel they are part of the learning environment. Knowledge of and sensitivity to a variety of cultural perspectives neither negates nor undermines the present canon. Tsehloane Keto emphasizes this need for variety when he says:

> The guard, however, should be on particularism. The input should be placing values on a shared power and centering of cultures, history and voices. The lure of hegemony is not only a temptation to Europe-centered scholarship. The Afrocentric perspective can also carry hegemonic undertones when all claims to progress in all regions of the world are explained in terms of the African presence and the African presence alone.[10]

Afrocentricity is not an exclusive world. The key is respect and inclusion. Nobelist Toni Morrison, who, according to the *New York Times*, is "the closest thing the country has to a national writer," makes an interesting corrective to hegemonic inquiry, revealing that it would be erroneous to

> ...alter one hierarchy in order to institute another. One should not want to encourage those totalizing approaches to African-American scholarship which have no drive other than the exchange of domination—dominant Eurocentric scholarship replaced by dominant Afrocentric scholarship.[11]

As Cornel West so accurately asserts, "The political challenge is to articulate universality in a way that is not a mere smoke screen for someone else's particularity. We must preserve the possibility of universal connection; that is the fundamental challenge."[12]

We should keep in mind that in order to center all cultures within the curriculum, whether the curriculum is European-centered, Asian-centered, African-centered, Hispanic-centered or First American-centered, we should avoid a hegemonic viewpoint.[14] For example, when curriculum leaders and book companies revise textbooks, they should keep a multifaceted mindset so that all cultures are placed within the text. A more holistic task would be for curriculum leaders and book companies to correct incorrect history.

IMPLICATIONS FOR ALL CULTURES

Educational centering does not create disunity nor does it "add on" nor is it about exclusiveness, domination, control, imperialism or replacement of one culture with

another. Rather, educational centering is inclusive because it values all peoples, and it is about solidifying the curriculum so that all cultures and historical data are infused within the curriculum. Cultural centering involves moving away from an exclusive Western-oriented curriculum, and placing children of color within the context of familiar cultural and social references. Molefi Asante defines "centering" as a term of location that attaches the student to the material in such a way that the student feels like part of the subject. This means one has to allow the character, the culture, and the personal and collective history bound within an individual to flow within in the learning environment. Knowledge of and sensitivity to cultures give hope to what a school, a church, a community or a world can be and should be. Therefore, educational centering is democratic, Christian, catholic, biblically oriented and universally embracing of all peoples as one.

Educational centering does not prefer one center to another, but embraces all centers as a way of viewing who God really is. As Father Cyprian Davis so discerningly put it: "God has many faces, and one of them is Black, one of them is White, one of them is Yellow, but all of them make for a rainbow circle of God's children."[14] The avenue to help initiate and bring about this holistic view of God is ethnic plurality participation in the curriculum from early childhood through the college level. This avenue is effective because culture is all-encompassing and plays an important role in the history of salvation.

Centering in education is a non-hierarchical approach that respects and celebrates a variety of cultural perspectives on world phenomena.[15] The fact that multiculturalism does not have a hegemonic outlook of the world and its cultures makes it inclusive. It centers Africans, Asians, Hispanics and Indians inside history and culture consciousness rather than outside of them. This pervasive idea presents the most revolutionary challenge to the ideology of world order.[16]

Multiculturalism maintains that in order for education to have integrity, one must begin with the position that all humans have contributed to world development, as well as to the flow of knowledge and information. Most achievements are the results of mutually active, international efforts. We need to dispel the myth that the West is homogeneous, that it owes few debts to other world civilizations.[17] James Weatherford describes the debt the West owes to the first Americans.[18] Martin Bernal, St. Clare Drake and Van Sertima, marshal considerable amounts of historical and cultural data to describe the ways in which African and Afro-Asiatic cultures influenced the development of Western civilization.[19] Bernal, for example, presents linguistic and archaeological evidence to substantiate his claim that important parts of Greek civilization (technologies, language, deities and architecture) originated in ancient Africa.

These concepts demonstrate why, without a multicultural education, students remain essentially ignorant of the contributions of a major portion of the world's people. A multicultural education is, therefore, a fundamental necessity for anyone who wishes to achieve competency in almost any subject.[20]

TEACHERS AS TRANSFORMERS OF KNOWLEDGE

Teachers have an awesome and tremendous capacity to bring spirituality and historical restorative empowerment to cultures that have remained unnamed and unknown within the walls of the classroom. As Elizabeth Minnich, in her discerning and engaging book, *Transforming Knowledge*, so adequately asserts:

As long as we do not engage in critique and correction of the curriculum, the framework of meaning behind particular questions of what to teach to whom will continue to prove inhospitable to all those who have been excluded from knowledge and knowledge making, and so from effective participation in understanding and exercising power on a basic cultural level.[21]

Before planning a lesson, teachers must first be centered in their own culture. Then they can proceed to place students within lessons so that each child feels he or she is an owner, not a renter, of knowledge. When every culture can be acknowledged within the walls of the classroom, church and the community, cultural relationships based on isolation and restraint will diffuse. What is proposed here

...is to examine the impact of notions of racial hierarchy, racial exclusion and racial vulnerability and availability on non-blacks who held, resisted, explored or altered those notions. The scholarship that looks into the mind, imagination and behavior of slaves is valuable. But equally valuable is a serious effort to see what racial ideology does to the mind, imagination and behavior of masters.[22]

In a monoethnic curriculum, children are left with a less-than-fulfilled and well-grounded learning of the worldview of other cultures. The curriculum may even choose to include the culture that seems most Western in its worldview and isolate the rest. Within these settings, world order is continually promoted and advanced. There are also "powerful and persuasive attempts to analyze the origin and fabrication of racism itself, contesting the assumption that it is an inevitable, permanent, and eternal part of all social landscapes."[23]

As evangelizers we have a greater call: the biblical call to be inclusive and to present the truth. The concern before us is that if the history of other cultures is not placed on equal terms, children become victims of not understanding exactly who all God's created people are. The isolated groups are viewed as "marginal" or "peripheral" beings. In other words, they become the "voiceless" who do not matter, "Invisible People" in the world order.

Said offers insightful ideology on the issues of essentialism and exclusiveness. He criticizes "theories of essentialism and exclusiveness," or "barriers and sides," for creating polarizations that condone ignorance and demagogy more than they promote knowledge. To him, such essentialist arguments are thus historical and oppressive at their core.

If you know in advance that the African, Chinese, Jewish or German experience is fundamentally integral, coherent, separate, and therefore comprehensible only to Africans, Chinese, Jews, or Germans, you first of all posit an essential something which is both historically created and the result of interpretation—namely the existence of Africanness, Chineseness, Jewishness, or Germanness....And secondly, you are likely, as a consequence, to defend the essence or experience itself rather than promote full knowledge of it and its entanglements and dependencies on other knowledge. As a result, you will demote the different experience of others to a lesser status.[24]

For world-order thinkers it does not matter how other cultures feel or, as singer Marvin Gaye stated, "what's going on" in their world. If world order is pleasing and satisfying to them, then all cultures should be satisfied. In promoting a holistic inclusion of the knowledge of history, religion, Church history, and the arts and sciences, teachers will help to construct a humanizing and spiritual community of faith. This

path will begin to change who and how we are in a world which we share with other cultures.

IMPLICATIONS FOR THE PARISH COMMUNITY

Yearly Pentecost Sunday celebrations, gatherings of Catholic school teachers and children and cathechetical conferences should be multicultural in scope and participation, with some symbolism of each culture placed within the environment of the church so that all cultures will feel accepted and welcome. This reaffirms what we confess and believe: that all cultures were brought forth out of the bosom of God. There is nothing shallow about this concept, nor is it a fringe concept. It is a God-centered concept. It is what we write about and talk about, and it still remains to be acted upon. Such gatherings will enable children, teachers and the Church to witness, and perhaps through this participation the issue of racism will begin to be erased from our schools, churches and communities. The same can be said about the other "isms"—classism and sexism. The solution for us as Christians is not more doctrines or rules; it is to bring to fruition what we believe and are encouraged to practice: that the word "catholic" is indeed universal and accepting.

A CHALLENGE FOR CATHOLIC UNIVERSITIES

On the college level, there are far too few colleges and universities that include the teaching of African religion, African spirituality (or at least the history of Black Catholics), African art and African literature. African religion has been greatly neglected by Western scholarship. Western scholars, with some few exceptions, have applied a "colonial mentality" or "dark-continent view" to African religion. The better textbooks on world religions treat African religions in the preliminary sections along with so-called "primitive religions" and then move on to "great religions." There has never been a text in the field that provides an adequate treatment of African or Native-American religions, yet elements of these religions have been borrowed, and these religions are beginning to be viewed as part of world order "great religion."

John Mbiti describes world-order views of African religions:

> It was believed that Africa borrowed many of its beliefs, characteristics and foods from the outside. All types of theories developed to explain how various religious traits reached Africans from the Middle East or Europe....The answer is that Africa has exported ideas, cultures and civilization to outsiders.[25]

Okot p'Bitek has also shared his view in this area. He believes that throughout the long history of Western scholarship, African religions have never been the object of study in their own right.[26] African deities were used as mercenaries in foreign battles, not one of which was in the interest of African peoples. Therefore, to define African religions as primitive is to give negative connotations to the word "African" in general. To hold such a superficial attitude toward African religions is to miss the fact that many aspects of traditional African religions are extremely rich and complex. Several of these aspects contain beliefs and practices which could shed light upon the study of all religions of the world.

The non-African scholar should avoid any conscious or unconscious assumption of superiority in studying African religions, because it only produces distortions. For

example, ethnographer Marcel Griaule sat and listened to the Dogon elder, Ogotemelli, for 23 days as he revealed the symbolic meaning of the highly complex cosmogony that Griaule had spent years trying to understand.[27]

Faculty members in the fields of theology, history, literature and philosophy are often ignorant of African-American philosophy, history, worldview, theology, literature, art, music and dance tradition. "Like thousands of avid but nonacademic readers, some powerful literary critics have never read, and are proud to say, any African-American text," observes Morrison.[28] Furthermore, it is unthinkable for them to read "any work other than that which is similar to what they themselves were taught in graduate school."[29]

African Catholic scholars look for centers in which to deposit their scholarly work within the walls of these universities, but the avenues of inclusion are not opened to them. This is important, because every intellectual gatherer occupies an identifiable center or location that provides an operational perspective affecting, when honestly pursued, the focus of gathered social data in all the human sciences.[30] As Keto says, "Scholars who are intellectual gatherers cannot study the actions of people on this planet without reference to a location or a center that is either overt or covert."[31] The hegemonic premises of many institutional locations will only allow scholarly work that is steeped in world-order ideology centers. Such colleges and universities promote peculiar and troubling beliefs.

Ultimately, professors at these locations cannot expand their analysis beyond a world-order point of view and may feel that knowledge has therefore been constrained or limited. This concern about hegemonic control of scholarship is verbalized through such phrases as: "But surely we should not teach work that is less than the best. Surely we should not lower our standard just to be inclusive."[32] But can the discourse of others be more fruitful? Here we see that it is not God's way that is important within these curriculums, it is the proclivity toward world order that is important.

As a result, this scholarship produces only partial knowledge for the community it is directed toward and should empower. As Minnich notes:

> It is partial in both senses of the term; it is actually about, and therefore tends strongly to work for, a part and not a whole. For example, the elaborate sets of theories as well as all that derives from them that we group under studies of "Western Civilization" tend very strongly to be partial insofar as they do not seriously take into account other civilizations except as they have been encountered by and then defined in relation to the dominant few of the West.[33]

If we know and understand Church history, for example, we know that Africa was Catholic before many other continents. Black Egypt, Nubia and Ethiopia gave the Church some of its finest leaders. Religious life as we have come to know it began on the continent of Africa. Because of the Moslem invasion, most of northern Africa became Islamic. However, a large number of the original Catholics came to settle in what we now know as the Bakongo (Zaire, Rwanda, Kenya) area. Even today that area is still heavily populated with Catholics.

In the 16th century, due to the kindness of Alfonso I, who invited the Franciscan missionaries to minister to his people, the Bakongo area flourished with Catholic monarchs. However, because of the onslaught of enslavement, African people were once more uprooted and were made to travel on slave ships to Hispaniola, which is now Haiti and the Dominican Republic.

Out of this melange, three forceful and spiritual women initiated a path of transcendency for the spiritual survival of their own people. Despite the horrors and debasement of enslavement in three key slave states, these African women transformed the environment and spiritual formation of their people. Who would have thought that Mother Lange, in founding the Oblate Sisters of Providence in Maryland, was performing a powerful creative act of grace?

Who would have thought that Delille's polyeclectic spirituality (Bakongo cosmology, Haitian cosmology and American Catholicism) would call her forth to debunk the laws of Louisiana in order to provide full and free grace in Louisiana's wilderness for her people and, at the same time, establish a community of black women that no European religious order in New Orleans wanted to be identified with?

Who would have thought that Mother Theodore Williams' forceful spirit and creative genius would outwit the Ku Klux Klan in order to establish a community in Georgia? Who would have thought that Pierre Toussant's liberating acts would challenge the attitude of his Christian slaveholder? Who would have thought that the leadership of Kentuckian Daniel Rudd (who later went to St. Louis) would challenge the hierarchy by calling them to live up to their principle of justice for all? And when they did not accept the challenge, Rudd and his associates did it themselves, propelling the First Black Catholic Congress into existence.

What is so poignant about all these examples is that any historian who wanted to document the formation of black Catholic communities in the United States would have to begin in those states where

If we know and understand Church history, we know that Africa was Catholic before many other continents.

black spiritual leaders moved and deposited their quintessence for the good of the Church and for the good of humanity. Once history is made, it cannot be denied. All of the above history and stories occurred during the enslavement period.[34] The question to be asked is: In what schools are these stories being told?

One of the most remarkable persons to have envisioned all cultures as local centers for empowerment was Mother Katharine Drexel. By witnessing the care that her mother showed to poor people of color, Katharine began to realize that all God's people are special, especially the poor. Locating herself within Gospel principles and her own holistic spirituality, Drexel heard the spirited call to liberate others. Drexel's reaction to viewing the "marginalized" as subjects and her concern for the cultures of others led her to choose a winding road that embraced all races. Drexel identified all God's people as human by her very life and voice. For Drexel, the Native and African Americans were the invisible cultures, unseen and unnoticed by the majority.

Even though she could have profited from world-order ideology because her family had the necessary resources, Katharine chose to live a life of challenge and possibilities for the sake of the Kingdom. By her very actions and verbal presentations, Katharine refused to give honor to the word "chattel" in reference to the Black and

Native American. Through these acts of grace, Katharine denounced the indifference, hostility and impassivity that characterized America's racist environment. Katharine Drexel did the right but not the most popular thing in establishing the Blessed Sacrament Sisters. In this manner, she propelled the Church community to correct the way they viewed Indians and Africans. The question to ask is: Where are the stories of these cultures in the religion text?

IMPLICATIONS FOR THE AFRICAN-AMERICAN STUDENT

In education, it means that teachers provide students with the opportunity to study the world and its people, concepts and history from an African worldview. In most classrooms, whatever the subject, European ideology and its worldview are located in the center of outlook. Teachers are desensitized to the presence of African children. How alien African children must feel and must have felt!

"As long as Black people are viewed as a 'them,' the burden falls on Blacks to do all the 'cultural' and 'moral' work necessary for healthy race relations. The implication is that only certain Americans can define what it means to be American—and the rest must simply 'fit in.'"[35] This statement by Cornel West is true in regard to imagery, views, perception of history, geography, mathematics, spirituality, science, music and art. One has only to visit a school where African-American children are the majority to witness the learning style, the imagery and the culture of the instructions that are placed there for African-American children to embrace. However, the hegemonic plague can work both ways if we are not assiduous in focusing on the perspective of many cultures. The same alienation would hold true if European, Asian or Hispanic children were to enter a school where imagery and lessons were only located in an exclusively African setting.

What is equally astounding is that little African children sit in classrooms and are taught in history classes to accept as heroes and heroines individuals who defamed African peoples. These students are being dislocated and decentered. For example, to have African children identify people living in the middle of the continent of Africa as "Middle Eastern" is decentering for African children. One may ask, Who are those nations "middle" to? Certainly not to the continent of Africa. Africa is made up of many nations, just as are other continents such as Asia, Australia and the Americas. There is nothing "middle" about any continent. This concept was the invention of world order in an effort to dislocate African peoples.

Purged ideologies of world history are at times used to empower one group of children over another. For example, according to linguist Martin Bernal:

> Whereas Greek civilization was known originally to have roots in Egyptian, Semitic, and various other southern and eastern cultures, it was redesigned as "Aryan" during the course of the nineteenth century, its semitic and African roots either actively purged or hidden from view. Since Greek writers themselves openly acknowledged their culture's hybrid past, European philologists acquired the ideological habit of passing over these embarrassing passages without comment, in the interests of Attic purity.[36]

This view insinuated itself within the hearts of the 19th-century disciples and discourses of intellectual pursuit. It was transformed to enslave and ostracize groups of people. And yet, history has revealed to us that "exclusion and devaluation of whole groups of people on the scale and of the range, tenacity, and depth of racism and sex-

ism and classism are systematic and shape the world within, where we all struggle to live and find meaning."[37] This is why the Jews have campaigned (and rightly so) to have the story of the European Holocaust taught in schools and colleges. Teaching about such monstrous human brutality should forever remind the world of the ways in which humans have often violated each other. Teaching about the African holocaust is just as important for many of the same reasons. When teaching about the enslavement period, teachers have to know who the Africans were and what gifts they brought to the American environment.

In a multicultural setting, teachers should not marginalize African-American students by causing them to question their own self-worth because their people's story is seldom told. By seeing themselves as subjects rather than objects of education—be the discipline biology, medicine, literature or social studies—African children will begin to see themselves not merely as seekers of knowledge, but as integral participants in it. Because all content areas are adaptable to a centering approach, African-American students can be made to see themselves as centered in the reality of any discipline.

If African, Asian and Native-American children must study European saints, then it should naturally follow that they must also know about and study the saints and holy people of their own cultures. If Asian, African and Native-American children must study the great European musicians, then they must know about the beginning of jazz, ragtime, African aesthetics, the spirituals and gospel music. All of these were not rooted in a purely American influence, but in an African influence.

Time is of the essence. We have an awesome and liberating task to implement. The key is to visualize the recognition and acknowledgement of a human and cultural continuum that incorporates and synthesizes diversity into the genesis of a uniquely American culture. As Minnich, in an engaging metaphor, tells us: "Old knots and tangles that are in all our minds and practices must be located and untied if there are threads available with which to weave the new into anything like a whole cloth, a coherent but by no means homogeneous pattern."[38]

Where we have relocated ourselves will determine the degree of difference we will make in how all cultures view the world. This is a "godly" task. What will be the sacred word?

NOTES

1. Toni Morrison, *Playing in the Dark,* New York, Vintage Books, 1992, p. 51.

2. Stephen May, *Making Multicultural Education Work,* Ontario, Toronto, Ontario Institute for Studies in Education, 1994, p. 7.

3. Paul Berman, *Debating P.C.: The Controversy over Political Correctness on College Campuses*, New York, Doubleday, 1992, p. 31.

4. Dinnish D'Souza, *Illiberal Education: The Politics of Race and Sex on Campus,* New York, The Free Press, 1991, pp. 12-15.

5. Ibid., p. 31.

6. Edward Said, *Culture and Imperialism,* New York, Alfred A. Knopf, 1993, p. 86.

7. Ibid., p. 93.

8. Lawrence Abbot, ed., *I Stand in the Center of the Good: Interviews with Contemporary Native American Artists,* Lincoln and London, University of Nebraska Press, 1994, pp. 71-72.

9. James Banks, *Teaching Strategies for Ethnic Studies,* Boston, Allyn and Bacon, 1991, p. 34.

10. Tsehloane Keto, *The African Centered Perspective in History,* Chicago, Research Associates School Times Publications, 1994, p. 70.

11. Morrison, op. cit., p. 8.

12. Cornel West, *Race Matters,* Boston, Beacon Press, 1993, p. 331.

13. Molefi Asante, *Afrocentricity,* Trenton, NJ, African World Press, 1987, p. 97.

14. Cyprian Davis, *Divine Word Missing,* Bay St. Louis, MS, 1984, p. 36.

15. Molefi Asante, "The Afrocentric Idea in Education," *Journal of Negro History,* vol. 60, no. 2, 1991, p. 173.

16. Ibid., p. 97.

17. Martin Bernal, *Black Athena: The Afroasiatic Roots of Civilization,* vol. 1, New Brunswick, NJ, Rutgers University Press, 1987, p. 34.

18. James Weatherford, *Indian Givers: How the Indians of the Americas Transformed the World,* New York, Facett Columbine, 1988.

19. Bernal, op. cit.; St. Clare Drake, *Black Folk Here and There,* vol. 1, Los Angeles, Center for Afro-American Studies, University of California, 1987; Van Sertima, *Black Women in Antiquity,* New Brunswick, NJ, Transaction Books, 1984.

20. Asante, op. cit., pp. 173-174.

21. Elizabeth Minnich, *Transforming Knowledge,* Philadelphia, Temple University, 1990, p. 12.

22. Ibid.

23. Morrison, op. cit., p. 11.

24. Said, op. cit., p. 31.

25. John Mbiti, *African Religions and Philosophy,* 2nd edition, Portsmouth, NH, Heinemann, 1990, pp. 6-7.

26. Okot p'Bitek, *African Religions in Western Scholarship,* Nairobi, East African Literature Bureau, 1971.

27. Marcel Griaule, *Conversation with Ogotemelli: An Introduction to Dogon Religious Ideas,* Oxford, Oxford University Press, 1965.

28. Morrison, op. cit., p. 13.

29. Minnich, op. cit., p. 12.

30. Keto, op. cit., p. 25.

31. Ibid., p. 13.

32. Minnich, op. cit., p. 99.

33. Ibid., p. 52.

34. Davis, op. cit., p. 36.

35. West, op. cit., p. 3.

36. Bernal, op. cit., pp. 230-236.

37. Minnich, op. cit., p. 33.

38. Minnich, op. cit., p. 36.

Additional Sources

Allen, P.G. *The Sacred Hoop: Recovering the Families in American Indian Traditions.* New York: Beacon Press, 1986.

American Black Catholic Bishops. "What We Have Seen and Heard," Cincinnati, Ohio, St. Anthony Messenger Press, 1984.

American Catholic Bishops. "Brothers and Sisters to Us." Washington, D.C.: USCC, 1984.

Coles, Robert. *Children of Crisis.* New York: Dell, 1964.

Davidson, Basil. *The African Past: Chronicles from Antiquity to Modern Times.* London: Longman, 1964.

Hannah, Arendt. *The Human Condition.* Chicago: University of Chicago Press, 1958.

Jameson, Frederic. *The Political Unconscious: Narrative as a Socially Symbolic Act.* New York: Cornell University Press, 1981.

McNeill, William H. *The Pursuit of Power: Technology, Armed Forces and Society Since 1000.* Chicago: University of Chicago Press, 1983.

Ottenberg, Simon and Phoebe, Eds. "The Idea of Person Among the Dogon." *Cultures and Societies of Africa.* New York: Random House, 1965.

Richard-Amoto, Patricia and Marguerite Ann Snow. *The Multicultural Classroom.* London, Longman, 1994.

——. *Orientalism.* New York: Pantheon, 1978.

Wilson, William. *The Truly Disadvantaged: The Inner City, the Underclass, and Public Policy.* Chicago: University of Chicago Press, 1987.

"Catechists and teachers must rigorously study culture, black expressive styles and behaviors if we are ever to reverse the pattern of sterile, repetitive, and maladaptive religious education modalities of faith and culture that simply don't work."

Nathan W. Jones, Ph.D.
Educator and Writer
From *Faith and Culture:
Multicultural Catechetical Resource*

"Little David, Play on Your Harp"

▲
▼

A Philosophy of Black Religious Pedagogy

▲
▼

Dr. Joseph A. Brown, SJ

Little David, play on your harp, Hallelu, Hallelu,
Little David, play on your harp, Hallelu;
Little David, play on your harp, Hallelu, Hallelu,
Little David, play on your harp, Hallelu.

Little David was a shepherd boy,
He killed Goliath and shouted for joy.
Little David, play on your harp, Hallelu, Hallelu, etc.
Joshua was the son of Nun,
He never would quit 'till his work was done.

Little David, play on your harp, Hallelu, Hallelu, etc.[1]

A Memoir

In East St. Louis, Illinois, in 1950, when I began my formal schooling, the city had already undergone several eras of historical significance: as an early site of abolitionist agitation (including the temporary freedom gate for Dred Scott); the race riots at the turn of the century; the great industrial and rail boom of the '30s and '40s; the harvest of culture to be exemplified by musicians such as Miles Davis, Clark Terry, Grant Green and the Turners (Ike and Tina); the great theatre luminary, Barbara Ann Teer; and others. Down the road at that time, in its near future, East St. Louis would see the meat-packing companies, the aluminum and glass manufacturers, and all the attending industries remove themselves almost overnight (in 1956 and thereafter). The city of wild living, rivaling New Orleans, Chicago, Kansas City or New York's uptown, Harlem, would collapse in upon itself, become a pallid grey and begin its chronic—if not fatal—bout with urban decay.[2]

The school to which I journeyed was part of a "mission to the colored" sponsored by the Society of African Missionaries, known universally in those days as the "White Fathers." The mission was dedicated to St. Augustine, and the school was staffed by the Dominican Sisters (of Sinsenawa, if my memory can be trusted). Many black Americans joined the Catholic Church in that area, especially during the 1930s, because of the aggressive commitment of some of the priests and nuns to evangelization and because of their involvement in social concerns. As would be true of many areas of the United States at that time, and would be true throughout the South and near-South of the country, those religious and clerics would have been outsiders to the region, in most cases.

St. Augustine Grade School housed eight grades in four classrooms. All of us students were black, and most were Catholic, either from the cradle or from school-age conversion. By 1954, the changes to the urban environment were already faintly present, and the St. Augustine Mission was closed and all its functions were shifted to St. Mary's Church and school. The priests, sisters, congregants and students all moved closer to the Mississippi River, to a much bigger physical plant and to a more congenial neighborhood. The perspective of childhood is probably universal in this regard: We adjusted instantaneously, because the human relationships were stable and the physical environment was of little regard. It just was.

The education I received in those first six grades of elementary schooling was as conservatively competent as could have been achieved anywhere. The test of this recollection was engaged when my family, as part of the economic exodus of the 1950s, moved to Beloit, Wisconsin, and my younger sister and I became the only two black children in the Catholic school system in that city. Neither of us lost an hour of adjustment to the curricular demands that might have been anticipated in our transferring from a poor black mission school in the south central Midwest, to the educational system supported by the middle- and upper-class Roman Catholic community in a small college town in the upper Midwest. We had the same level of intellectual preparation that was given to the (white) daughters and sons of shop stewards, waitresses, college professors, and factory owners. In 1956, we were *Catholic* first and *Negro* only afterward—at least in our eyes and in the eyes of our peers, at least initially.

What did I learn during my 12 years of Catholic school education? To read, to spell, to compute; to discover the economic riches of the world, through a study of geography; to develop an appreciation for the fine and performing arts, through the study and practice of music, drama, writing and drawing. We were still in the age where hearing stories read aloud was an expected treat on Friday afternoons. I was encouraged to make use of a library card for the public library. We were placed in a diocesan children's choir and performed several times a year. We were obliged for daily attendance at Mass and immersed in the prodigal abundance of the rituals in the old Roman calendar. Why shouldn't young black children in a drug-infested urban setting learn to pray with Italian and Romanian and Nigerian children during the celebration of the Rogation Days? Why should we not be bused to yet another revival of "The Song of Bernadette"? Why should we not be spiritually aroused with the stories of St. Agnes and Tarcisius and Angela Merici; of Martin de Porres and Rose of Lima; of Miguel Pro and the Jesuit martyrs of North America? We were still at the age where mystical identification was the basis of our prayer and the fuel for our spirituality. We learned to be Catholics, according the piety available to us, in the classroom, in the church, everywhere. Few of us, at that time, could have dis-

cerned the subtext of our instruction, could have articulated any submerged intuition that we were objects of evangelization, instruction, and catechesis, and not subjects of disinterested service. But somewhere, the difference was noted.

For me the epiphany came during the fourth grade, a point at which, I have since learned, is a threshold in all early learning. Migraine headaches (which had begun in the second grade) intensified their onslaught; rashes and bouts of depression and anxiety, leading to other physical illnesses, became common. When lecturing on this topic, I can generate much laughter and signs of wistful remembrance when I describe my first "spiritual crisis," concerning our weekly fundraising activities for the The Society of the Holy Childhood and its campaign for the ransoming of "pagan babies." The only humor that seems to actually derive from this recollection is based on the natural balance time provides all memories. In the main, because the memory is instructive, it is neither painful nor jocose.

On the occasion in question, while looking through one of the magazines provided to publicize the heroic efforts of missionaries at work on the continent of Africa (and elsewhere around the globe), listening with the one distracted ear most students grow at an early age, I was caught up in an epiphanic moment: The pagan babies being referred to in the articles before me, and in the exhortation being delivered in front of us, *were* us; my eye beheld our otherness, in a manner worthy of the best of the "observing observed" who might be studied in contemporary anthropology. A quiet resolve seeped into my consciousness (and the memory I inscribe here was part of my nine-year-old consciousness; of this I am certain) and my outward show of solidarity with the heathen children across the ocean took on unexpected affinities, and shaped my sense of church and mission forever afterward. I knew that,somewhere, some child was looking at a picture of me while being encouraged to donate funds for my salvation. How could I send money for my own redemption?

"Anybody ask you who you are, who you are, who you are;
Anybody ask you who you are, you tell them: 'I'm a child of God.'"

FORGING A WAY OUT OF NO WAY

Throughout the history of the black community in the United States, individual and communal initiatives (by black and white alike) toward the securing of the tools and benefits of education are legendary and heroic in tenacity and scope. The continuous efforts to deny such opportunities for educational advancement are proof of the deep-rooted desire for black people to educate themselves. From the bombing of Prudence Crandall's school in Connecticut, in 1833, to the establishment—by black people—of the Savannah Educational Association in Savannah, Georgia, during the Civil War, prophetic and devoted men and women, black and white, have risked death to provide schooling for black children. Black children, and their elders, were not passively waiting for schools to present themselves, we must remember. The multitude of laws prohibiting the instruction of slaves, and the stark and always vicious methods of punishing those enslaved Africans who were found to be literate, all give witness to the widespread phenomenon of the black enslaved desiring to be literate and free. In a peculiar spiritual context, in some "slave narratives," we can find accounts of African Americans who sought the help of God, or were the direct beneficiaries of such divine aid, in acquiring skills of literacy.[4] In this regard, what

may be the most famous case of a combination of divine favor and individual grace-filled action is found in the autobiographical writings of Frederick Douglass. Within the passage of Douglass' *Narrative,* where he described the revelation of the "pathway from slavery to freedom," we may find the seeds of successful and ineffective pedagogies in the education of black youth.

Around the age of seven, Frederick Douglass was sent from the plantation where he was born into the city of Baltimore, where he resided in the home of Mr. and Mrs. Thomas Auld for nearly seven years. During those years, Douglass learned to read and write. In accomplishing this goal, Douglass "was compelled to resort to various stratagems." The "living word of faith and spirit of hope" sustaining him in this "pathway from slavery to freedom" were based on an injunction forbidding Douglass access to instruction. These words of his master to his mistress, fortuitously overheard by Douglass, served as an ironic revelation, a light piercing the darkness of Douglass' ignorance. The ignorance did not concern the instruction itself; rather, as long as Douglass was ignorant of the motive behind the denial of access, he could not fashion a strategy to overcome the obstacle of illiteracy. The reasoning of Thomas Auld, far from being an aberration found in the mind of a blatantly racist slaveowner, actually contained much hardheaded realism, and displayed (in Douglass' rendering of the account) a prescient outline of the social worth of education, then and now. Douglass obviously recognized the wisdom of Auld's sanction, and was thereby fortified with a philosophical insight that would free him to educate himself, according to the inverse of his master's wishes.

> ...Mr. Auld found out what was going on, and at once forbade Mrs. Auld to instruct me further, telling her, among other things, that it was unlawful, as well as unsafe, to teach a slave to read. To use his own words, further, he said, 'If you give a nigger an inch, he will take an ell. A nigger should know nothing but to obey his master—to do as he is told to do. Learning would spoil the best nigger in the world. Now,' said he, 'if you teach that nigger (speaking of myself) how to read, there would be no keeping him. It would forever unfit him to be a slave. He would at once become unmanageable, and of no value to his master. As to himself, it could do him no good, but a great deal of harm. It would make him discontented and unhappy.'[5]

What does this passage tell us about the state of education in America, in the 19th and 20th centuries, as it relates to the realities of black children, enslaved or poor, free or financially secure? First, we must remember that formal schooling does nothing to prepare an individual to be an agent of social change. On the contrary, all educational theorists, from Plato (in *The Republic*) to John Dewey, describe the most effective systems of education as vehicles to prepare the young to be productive members of whatever society already exists and which uses the school for the transmission of its cultural values. All formal schooling in the 19th century could have done for the likes of Frederick Augustus Washington Bailey (Douglass' name at the time) would have been to teach him that he could never hope to be a citizen of America, that he could never participate fully in the representative democracy that both sustained and depended upon the world of chattel slavery. To permit Douglass, or any slave, to read the Bible in its entirety would be to expose him to notions of deliverance from slavery as profound and as concrete as any example from history. To place before the mind of this enslaved child the great words of Paine, Voltaire, Shakespeare, Jefferson or Franklin would be to infect him with dreams of freedom

and independence that would be fatal to his narrowly circumscribed situation.

Auld was, in his own way, generous in his concerns: To teach this boy—or any of the enslaved—to read would be "against the law," because it would be the direct fostering of social discontent. Law exists to maintain good order. Formal systems of education provide instruction as to an individual's proper response to the rules and traditions of one's particular society, and of "civilization" in general. As many of the enslaved would have said and would have found agreement from the more truthful of the masters, the law did not apply to the enslaved. How could one, for instance, be prosecuted for stealing property when one was considered property, and had been gained through an act of thievery originally?[6]

The very notion of a "good nigger," crystallized in Auld's words, depends on a thoughtless, disconnected creature, whose imagination has been stunted, whose sense of morality has been coerced into compromise and acts of desperation. In short, once Douglass—at the age of seven—realized that reading would reconstitute him into personhood, he embarked upon a spirited (and spirit-possessed) endeavor to make himself anything but a slave. Because he wished to end his discontent, he took control of his education.

> It was a new and special revelation, explaining dark and mysterious things, with which my youthful understanding had struggled, but struggled in vain. I now understood what had been to me a most perplexing difficulty—to wit, the white man's power to enslave the black man. It was a grand achievement, and I prized it highly. From that moment, I understood the pathway from slavery to freedom. It was just what I wanted, and I got it at a time when I the least expected it.[7]

Through and beyond all the ironies exploding in Douglass' narrative, we must keep sight of one deep-rooted truth: Whatever great themes of emancipation, justice, the privileges of individual freedom or the triumph of the law that Douglass may have discovered in the pages of the *Columban Orator* and similar works, the reality of blackness was inescapable—no matter how much schooling he could wrest or steal for himself, he would never be a part of a democratic society. In 1857, more than ten years after Douglass published his *Narrative,* the Chief Justice of the Supreme Court asserted, among other matters of law:

> In the opinion of the [Supreme] court, the legislation and histories of the times, and the language used in the Declaration of Independence, show, that neither the class of persons who had been imported as slaves, nor their descendants, whether they had become free or not, were then acknowledged as a part of the people, nor intended to be included in the general words used in that memorable instrument.[8]

Once Douglass—at the age of seven—realized that reading would reconstitute him into personhood, he embarked upon a sprited (and spirit-possessed) endeavor to make himself anything but a slave.

Further along in this judgment known as the *Dred Scott Decision,* Taney stated that no matter where an enslaved person might travel in the United States, freedom was not possible; therefore citizenship was inherently denied the enslaved and their descendants. It took a bloody war to overturn that legal opinion. The principles of law and tradition which could nourish such thinking, historically, have not vanished from the contemporary thinking of many of the designers and arbiters of law and custom in the land. Our educational systems generally fail today, as they failed in the days of Douglass, Scott, Auld and Taney, to prepare those who would challenge and transform society. Such a conclusion cannot be an indictment of the public school system, since, as John Dewey instructed the nation: "[Education] gives individuals a personal interest in social relationships and control, and the habits of mind which secure social changeswithout introducing disorder."[9]

Frederick Douglass, while he is often held up as a role model based on his heroic resistance to the system of slavery, and because of his incomparable accomplishments in literature and philosophy, cannot be taught as an exemplar of the successful student in the public school systems (nor, if the argument to be developed here has any validity, in the Catholic parochial school systems) of the United States. Douglass broke all the laws then in existence, and dedicated himself to seizing power from those who controlled his life and the commerce of society; and that by any means necessary. While Douglass stands, in the minds of some, as the representative "self-made" black person, he also stands as someone who knew himself to be incapable of citizenship in the republic as it stood. He was, in many ways, "in the world, but not of it."

His education, as described in the *Narrative* and elsewhere, had components worthy of our consideration today, if we are to put our creative energies into renewing the Catholic educational system for the benefit of the African-American community. The first element was, as mentioned, *formal schooling.* Douglass used the lessons of Mrs. Auld, and supplemented them with further *skill training gained subversively* through his involvement with school boys "on the street." Through psychological games and manipulations of their egos, Douglass convinced other children to share their formal knowledge with him, in decidedly informal settings.

> As many of these [little white boys whom I met in the street] as I could, I converted into teachers. With their kindly aid, obtained at different times and in different places, I finally succeeded in learning to read. When I was sent on errands, I always took my book with me, and by going one part of my errand quickly, I found time to get a lesson before my return. I used also to carry bread with me, enough of which was always in the house, and to which I was always welcome; for I was much better off in this regard than many of the poor white children in our neighborhood. This bread I used to bestow upon the hungry little urchins, who in return, would give me that more valuable bread of knowledge.[10]

Douglass first used his basic peer identity for *solidarity,* then appropriated a class advantage for establishing a *system of reward* for services rendered. Finally he engaged a sympathy for fairness and justice, found in all young people, by pointing out during these lessons that, while his erstwhile pedagogues would be "free as soon as [they would be] twenty-one," he would be a slave for life. *Reciprocal education* was taking place, at his initiative.

These characteristics of his self-determined quest for an education were repeated throughout his life. By the time he was about twelve years old, he had gained a profi-

ciency in literacy. He discovered that this knowledge did indeed make him fearfully discontent. His clandestine reading crowded his imagination with futile dreams of escape and freedom. At the first stage of his education, he was frustrated because he was alone in his situation. After he was sent back to the plantation country in Maryland, he was able to find kindred restless souls, and he once again proved the pragmatic value of the education he had acquired. Douglass reinforced his conviction that education must be used, in his universe, to *subvert the established order*. In his dealings with his fellow enslaved, he made much use of his ability to read and write by providing forged documents, by which they could gain temporary mobility and limited freedom. He deceived the often illiterate and always white patrollers who acted as mercenary police helping to control the enslaved population and thwart the phenomenon of runaways. On a level of irony quite prevalent in Douglass' writings, he withheld information and deceived those who could have been the adult versions of the "hungry little urchins" who had helped him gain his knowledge, years before. When he was once again a part of African culture, he placed his skills at the disposal of the community. Education for service and betterment are long-standing requirements of black education, it seems.

The last element of Douglass' education that demands our attention is the cultural. From many textual evidences, we can see the breadth of his reading among the classics available to the most well-educated 19th century scholars. Greek and Roman history and philosophy; Scripture studies; the works of Shakespeare; the abundance of contemporary political and literary thought concerning justice and freedom—knowledge of all these appears in his autobiographies, essays and speeches. He had dipped his soul in this river of knowledge long before he attempted a physical escape from enslavement. And his first attempts failed.

Frederick Douglass established his own prototypical double consciousness when he reflected on why his first conspiracy to escape failed. Some of the failure was due to the "Judas factor" of a member of the conspiracy turning informant; some was due to an inadequate preparation and consideration of the complexities of successful escape. Douglass added another factor to his recollection—he was not spiritually in readiness; but in doing so, only partially revealed the substantial role played by his penultimate mentor in literacy.[11]

As a direct consequence of his learning, Douglass proved Mr. Auld's prophecy true: He was, after a time, "unfit to be a slave" and was sent to the care of Mr. Covey, a notorious slave breaker, who nearly succeeded in breaking Douglass in mind, soul, body and spirit. After months of undergoing degrading, sadistic violence at the hands of Covey, Douglass made his way over dozens of miles to present his condition to his master, still in Baltimore. He was forced to return to Covey. Entering Covey's yard, Douglass suddenly bolted and hid in the forest. This "run to the wilderness" is a classic scene in the slave narratives and in all black spirituality. The woods, the valley, the wilderness, the mountaintop—all are places where the individual must go for a mystical education, for a direct encounter with the divine. No earthly knowledge is sufficient for liberation (or salvation) if there is not this refinement of mystical strength. It is in the mystical space—"way up in the middle of the air"— that the person discovers that there is a larger reality than that experienced daily in servitude and despair, and this reality is bounded by the "horizon of God." For every "motherless child, a long ways from home," there must be "a rock in a weary land" in order for the "poor, wayfaring stranger" to have the courage to continue traveling

in "a cold and friendless world." Until Jesus experienced the 40 days in the desert (reenacting the journey of Moses into the clouds of Mount Sinai), he could not know the depths of himself. Solitary prayer and fasting are the necessary preludes to human completion. The "wilderness" is the schoolroom of the soul and every school must have a teacher. For Douglass, it was Sandy Jenkins.

> I spent that day mostly in the woods, having the alternative before me—to go home and be whipped to death, or stay in the woods and be starved to death. That night I fell in with Sandy Jenkins, a slave with whom I was somewhat acquainted. ...I went home with him, and talked this whole matter over, and got his advice as to what course it was best for me to pursue. I found Sandy an old adviser.[12]

Douglass went into the woods, looking for Sandy Jenkins. The "old adviser" was a disguised "conjure man," and someone Douglass trusted with his life. When he was at his lowest, and all of his stratagems had failed, he sought help from one of his elders. At such a time in his life, it was obvious he would not talk the whole matter over with someone who would be of no help. Sandy Jenkins pushed Douglass into a new realm of behavior—and into a world that is surprising to be found in a text that otherwise speaks in the heightened rhetoric of the Romantic age.

> He told me, with great solemnity, I must go back to Covey; but that before I went, I must go with him into another part of the woods, where there was a certain root, which, if I would take some of it with me, carrying it always on my right side, would render it impossible for Mr. Covey, or any other white man, to whip me.[13]

After making a few textual demurrals, which sound quite unconvincing, Douglass tells his readers that he followed Sandy Jenkins' advice, returned to confront Covey, withstood his threats by a show of force on his own part, and was never again threatened—by Covey or anyone else. Frederick Douglass then, after one other aborted attempt at escape, followed more of Sandy Jenkins' advice, and made his way to legal freedom. He had put himself under the tutelage of an *African griot,* who taught him the ways of the woods (quite helpful, one would imagine, in making one's way out of slavery), the ways of discerning human nature, the ways of reliance on his spiritual gifts; and who taught him to rely on the secret knowledge that is coded in the culture of African Americans everywhere: He must carry his root with him always.

OH, WHAT A BEAUTIFUL CITY/TWELVE GATES TO THE CITY

We will now perform a rapid survey of some of the major characteristics of the traditional role of U. S. Catholic schools in the formation of the young, with some attention paid to what can be called the "triple motive" of schooling. Catholic immigration into North America, no matter the cultural origin of the immigrating population, had some distinguishing features. As will be readily seen, these features are in an almost dialectical opposition to the experiences of our African ancestors, who were the largest group of unwilling immigrants in world history.

The first wave of immigration was due to exploration and conquest. The Spanish and French explorers brought with them clerics who had two primary tasks: to minister to the explorers and to evangelize among the indigenous population. After a measure of conquest provided a stable environment, the second wave of immigration

was possible. The importation of women, who brought with them the cultural imperatives necessary for permanent residence, necessitated the next development of religious activity. Churches, schools and hospitals (social service organizations) had to be established. On the ships of the French and Spanish and English Catholics, from 1540 to 1740, were to be found clerics and religious women and men from every region and country of Europe, representing every distinct population of immigrants found in the New World. Catholics came to America already Catholic, and brought with them the men and women capable of replicating the religious and social organizations necessary for the quickest possible establishment of a hospitable cultural milieu. Since these earliest immigrants were able to establish these hospitable environments and establish a clear dominance of land and resources, the cultures that flourished were as hegemonic as could be expected. When the next wave of Catholic immigration occurred, mainly in the 19th century, the cities that stood ready to absorb the "huddled masses, yearning to breathe free" already had in place complex networks of churches, schools, orphanages and relief societies—but only for the established "old guard."

The Irish, German, East European, Italian, Basque and other Catholic immigrants, most of whom were driven to the United States by the economic chaos induced by political unrest, were penned into restricted urban settings or migrated to rural areas evocative of the landscapes left behind. Into each of these locales they brought with them their own clergy, an educated class of "elders" who served as the mediators, guides, arbiters and fixed points on the compasses, needed for survival in the teeming cities of America. The clergy, and the churches they erected immediately, also served as links with the cultures left behind. The Eucharistic liturgies and devotional life of these Catholic communities maintained the native languages, the pious customs, the manners and traditions of the Old World, providing comfort in the chaos,and mediating institutions which could provide transitions for the first generation of immigrants. The Germans, Irish, Lithuanians, Sicilians, Poles, Alsatians and other European Catholics came to America as Catholics. Upon arriving they discovered patterns of religious behavior that were sufficiently similar to what they brought with them. They also brought with them a (more or less) educated clergy, who were able to immediately plug into a hierarchical society that gave them the political and social leverage their congregations desperately needed for survival. The "faith" was familiar.

But the American world was not as homogeneous for this generation of Catholic immigrants as might have been the case for the earlier transplants. While all-English or all-Spanish or all-French communities could have been possible in 1590 or 1632, by 1840 or 1880 or 1912, the newly arriving Catholics had to rub shoulders with men and women of every culture and creed found on the earth. The shoulder-rubbing could often be abrasive, if not life-threatening, for political and economic reasons too numerous and well-known to mention here. The schools created during this era are the schools we have inherited and that we struggle to maintain today, as "Catholic schools." The rationale of these schools provides the triple motive of Catholic education that I suggest was the glory of the Catholic cultures of America, and which has been nearly lost in the urban environments of today.

The first motive has been described already. The schools were established *to maintain cultural and religious integrity* for the first and second generations of immigrant families. The "root" faith of the old world was sustained and taught to the children born on this side of the Atlantic. The devotion to the saints of the old soil,

the songs, the feasts and festivals of the birth culture were practiced and privileged in the new settings. Since the children of these newly arrived would not have been allowed into the established Catholic schools because of prejudices unworthy of any Christians—and universal to all societies—and because public schools were not viable options, each language community provided its own schools, in order to keep the sense of community as strong as possible. The schools were built, also, to enable the children brought and born into the New World *to become socialized for effective inclusion* into the cultural marketplace that is America.

In this regard there was a double focus in the education given and received in these school settings. Language skills and civics lessons were poured into the young. At the same time, the "tenets of the faith" were drilled into the souls of the students in these schools. A child might be instructed to lose his accent, but no one would allow him to lose his faith. A young woman might be taught the social manners necessary for working outside the neighborhood, but she would be armored in the faith, lest she forget "where she came from." If the community could not afford an independent parochial school, the religious and moral instruction would take place in the home or in the church, without exception. It was a matter of life-or-death urgency that each child be fortified against the snares of the wicked, who were to be found everywhere in the cities of "otherness." *Effective inclusion* meant that the child might learn what was necessary to be "American" but must also be reminded of what it meant to be "Catholic." *Catholic,* of course, had a different flavor, a different rhythm, a different costume, a different panoply of protective saints in each church, in each neighborhood.

> ▲
> ▼
>
> *Catholic had a different flavor, a different rhythm, a different costume, a different panoply of protective saints in each church, in each neighborhood.*
>
> ▲
> ▼

The third motive for the establishment of the Catholic school system was *to provide a seedbed for religious and clerical vocations.* This aspect of Catholic education is seldom highlighted today, but it is of paramount importance in any reflection on the golden age of Catholic schools. Social services were often nonexistent in the public sphere, in most of the United States. Because of anti-Catholic sentiment in most of the country throughout the 19th and early 20th centuries, Catholics were responsible for building and sustaining all the social organizations necessary for their well-being and security. Insurance societies, orphanages, homes for abused women, old-age homes, charitable-help organizations, the schools themselves—if these organizations were to be kept in place within the community, they would have to be staffed and controlled in the most effective manner possible. The solution to this problem also arrived on the boats with the immigrants. The religious women and men who had vowed themselves to service of the community, under the protection of the Church, were primarily responsible for the building of American Catholic cultural institutions. If a bishop needed a school for his diocese and could not import religious men or women to support such an endeavor, he would often create a religious community locally.

The expectation remained high into the 1950s that the Catholic community would provide the human resources for the establishment of these necessary institutions. This expectation was nourished by the continued power of the two previous motives. The presupposition that one could lose one's faith in the marketplace meant that there was a critical need for an *apologetic* catechesis as part of the total schooling of the Catholic young. During the 1930s, '40s and '50s, this motive was bolstered by the obsessive anti-Communism found everywhere in the U. S. Catholic Church. Catholic colleges and universities flourished, often as one last effort to keep young adults "protected" from Protestants, atheists and Communists, while also providing an education that would make them socially and economically competitive with, often, the very same people.

Religious vocations were naturally progressive, in this world. By this I mean that young men and women were selected out, at an early age, as likely candidates for privileged work (service) in the community. It was almost exclusively through the Catholic school system that this process was carried to harvest. The family, the church, the school—the entire community—gave pride of place to those who would keep the community, the church, the school sacred and safe for the future. The Catholic community, like every institution everywhere, had within its structures certain mechanisms to provide for its continuance. Any young woman who was especially gifted academically or who displayed an interest in any of the "helping professions" (teaching, nursing, social work, etc.) would be confronted with the question of a vocation. The same pattern held true for young men. Those who were above average academically or who demonstrated sensitivity in the various ritual opportunities available only to them or who were less aggressively socialized according to stereotypes of maleness, would be singled out and nurtured by a variety of mentors, all under the rubric of "fostering vocations."

The vocation to religious or clerical life was, then, a vocation to leadership and to the maintenance of cultural and religious institutions. Within such a maintenance was the supposition that much of the work would be to educate the targeted population to better fit into the larger social universe.

"SOMETIMES I FEEL LIKE A MOTHERLESS CHILD"

From the preceding discussion, it should be readily apparent that the triple motives ascribed to Catholic schools in this essay could not be easily actualized in the efforts to educate children of African descent, at any time in the history of the United States. We need only remind ourselves that the Church's relationship with Africans in the New(er) World was as problematic as its dealings with Africa had been in the "Older World." The exploration, development and domination of the Americas soon depended on the African slave trade, and the clerics who blessed and sanctioned the conquest of "Eldorado" or "the New Eden" or the "New Jerusalem" inevitably submitted to the reality of slavery.

Representatives of all the Christian churches, including those such as the Quakers, Methodists, Dominicans, Franciscans, and Jesuits, who had at one time or another railed against the enslavement of the Native Americans, eventually accommodated themselves to the point where every group just mentioned profited over time from the trading of enslaved men and women. The economy and the political structures created to protect the economic well-being of the country demanded that

all who would be Americans would, in some measure, be forced to deal with chattel slavery as the bedrock of the republican democracy that governed the nation.

This conscious accommodation to slavery and to the philosophy of racism that justified the continuance of *racial oppression of some for the benefit of others* is, in some ways, one of the necessary tests of one's ability to claim one's identity as an American. For in the foundational scheme of American cultural identity, full person-hood, and full citizenship, could be claimed only by white males who could own or acquire property. No one illuminates this phenomenon more eloquently than James Baldwin, in the introduction to his collected nonfiction, *The Price of the Ticket*. Baldwin alluded to the fact that the "Christian state" of America made "pragmatic decisions concerning Property sometime ago," and that all immigrants who arrived in America had to confront the fact that the control of human *labor* and capital involved defining some human beings to be *property,* or *capital*. Those who were not so defined were granted their status only in relation to those who were so defined. There was an urgency to claim a new identity. But all had to "pay the price of the ticket" for the privilege of becoming American, of becoming *white:*

> [the generality of white Americans] come through Ellis Island, where *Giorgio* becomes *Joe, Pappavasiliu* becomes *Palmer, Evangelos* becomes *Evans, Goldsmith* becomes *Smith* or *Gold,* and *Avakian* becomes *King.* So, with a pain-less change of name, and in the twinkling of an eye, one becomes a white American. Later, in the midnight hour, the missing identity aches. One can neither assess nor overcome the storm of the middle passage. One is mysteriously ship-wrecked forever in the Great New World.[14]

Baldwin is attempting, here and throughout his work, to bring the witness of the true history of America before the eyes of those who feel compelled to deny it. It is this special condition of racism that makes the problems of African Americans in this country the irreducible "stumbling block" by which justice is wounded daily. It is this quality, this "price," that gives to recent immigrants the permission to despise or devalue the African Americans upon whom they depend for their economic suc-cess. The spectacle of a Korean shopowner calling an African-American adolescent a "nigger," as happened famously in Los Angeles in 1992, illustrates this point quite well and provides another example of Baldwin's thesis, especially when he says:

> The Irish middle passage, for but one example, was as foul as my own, and as dishonorable on the part of those responsible for it. But the Irish became white when they got here and began rising in the world, whereas I became black and began sinking. The Irish, therefore and thereafter—again, for but one example—had absolutely no choice but to make certain that I could not menace their safety or status or identity; and, if I came too close, they could, with the consent of the governed, kill me. Which means that we can be friendly with each other anywhere in the world, except Boston.[15]

Remembering the second suggested motive for the Catholic school means that we must admit the reality that all too often these attitudes equating black with menace, threat and danger were (and, in some places, still may be) taught as part of the cur-riculum of assimilation. The theological support for racism had long been estab-lished, with some of the dedicated and heroic religious men and women who labored in the vineyard of the American Church utilizing an endowment of slaves in order to support their ministry. The daughters and sons of the well-established first wave of

immigrants, those who established their domination of early Catholic settlements in the United States, often went to their boarding schools with their personal "body servants" as part of their entourage. We can well imagine that these "servants" acquired superior educations in the same subversive manner as was employed by Frederick Douglass. We must at the same time remember that these black men and women were invisible participants in Catholic schooling, by the deliberate denials of their presence.

Given the nature of cultural prejudice—a prejudice that, first, gave the nation its economy and peculiar sense of justice; and, second, precipitated the bloody Civil War, because of the otherwise invincible evil of the system—it is impossible for us to conceive that many African Americans could have been the full beneficiaries of a Catholic school education during the first 150 years of United States history. The argument that would introduce the pioneering work of the Oblate Sisters of Providence, who opened a school for black children in 1828, or the great contributions of the Sisters of the Holy Family, whose network of black Catholic schools began in 1867, can modify the claims made here, only slightly. No one who graduated from those—or other "black"—schools could ever be the equals of the immigrant Catholics who were not African. The schools for black Catholics would provide religious instruction, competent schooling in the arts and sciences, and support for community development—but only within the restricted segregated society allowed to black Americans, generally. The terminal point for such an education was not assimilation into America, but advancement to the ranks of *elite* African Americans. Of course, the fervent *hope* of all those African men and women who created and endowed these schools for the stabilization and development of their communities was that someday, somewhere, somehow, their children would prove to the larger world their worth and right to freely participate in American society as equals of white citizens. But within the Catholic cultures that formed the Church in the United States, that hope was distant and dim.[16]

The third motive for Catholic education—the development of vocations for the continuance of the work of the faith community—brings us to the most glaring place where the schools would have inherently failed. We must acknowledge that the educational enterprise of Catholic schools among the black community could never have been completely successful. Just as Mr. Auld, in the story of Frederick Douglass' quest for literacy, might be viewed as providing a tortured and guilt-laden testimony to the all-encompassing nature of racism, so too did many of the dedicated nuns and brothers and priests who controlled the Catholic schools have to admit that the impulse to foster vocations had to be suppressed, when focused upon young black women and men. One era of Church people compromised with slavery, thereby setting the stage for another era's compromise in the face of the structural racism permeating all facets of society—religious and secular.

It could not have been otherwise. Countless "faithful Catholics" had been taught, as part of the price of the ticket of becoming American (i.e., *white*), that all black people were in all ways inferior to any white people. How could they then conceive of a Church where they would be taught doctrine; have the sacraments administered to them; receive guidance, counseling or direction for their secular lives and for their heavenly salvation by creatures who were to be otherwise despised, rejected or eradicated according to the greater good of "real" people, "real" citizens, "real" Catholics? How, in other words, could a pagan baby ever become a bishop? "Sister" to whom? "Father" for whom?

For the black participants in the Catholic school system, generally, assimilation was but a distant, romantic dream—with *absorption* or *adoption* possible only for the one or two special, exceptional individuals who proved to the larger world how *unlike* other blacks they were. The faith that was to be refined and kept inviolate was not an issue for African peoples, who had been judged to be without culture, without faith, without any of the gifts of civilization brought to these shores as heirlooms by other immigrant populations. No; for the black children, the issue never arose. The "one true faith" was deemed alien to African peoples, and the various cultural interpretations of Roman Catholicism that would have been part of the inheritance of the various missionaries were the real treasures, to be deposited into the empty vessels among whom they labored. Once the work of evangelization had been attempted, it would have been truncated, since the fullness of evangelization—in the popular theology of American Catholicism before the 1960s—would have terminated in a religious or priestly vocation, which was another impossible goal for all but the most exceptional African-American individuals to achieve.

What often developed, then, was a sense of *service as sacrifice*, a theology of *uplift* of the colored masses. Much of the education traditionally available to African Americans in the Catholic schools of the United States might appear similar to the attempt of Mrs. Auld to teach young Frederick Douglass his ABCs. Douglass, even with the passing of many years, remembered her as an angelic presence, opening his life to the limitless possibilities closed to him before. The intervention of harsh social and political realities (the voice of Mr. Auld, the concerns of the racist state) circumscribed the achievement of those possibilities for all but the few who, like Frederick Douglass, glimpsed a light in the midst of nearly overwhelming darkness.

In the past missionary endeavors of Catholic schooling, often the effort was all, since there was little prospect of the school being able to change the larger reality of racism. But we must turn our gaze to the mountaintop, whence cometh our salvation, and ask, "Shall these bones live?" We must ask what is possible for the Catholic school today, and tomorrow? And will there even be Catholic schools in the black community tomorrow? If there are to be schools, what can they provide, to redeem the past—when more was not possible, for a variety of internal and external reasons? If there are to be schools, then what must the focus of the instruction be?

The answers, of course, have been the yeast which has leavened this text, thus far. Can we learn from those who have successfully educated themselves and others, and use their wisdom and experience to renew the face of the Catholic school system?

The "motherless child" must find a refuge and a home and become as valuable as any of the great heroes of the Bible, sung about in the spirituals. Little David, playing on his harp, might be a good example of how we might adapt the pedagogy set forth in the story of Frederick Douglass, and once again provide the education our students need to survive in a world that is still as harsh and cruel as any ever seen.

"Tell Them You're a Child of God"

Most children are born into the world at the top of their game, genius level. The culture that receives them will either nurture and develop the genius in them or silence their minds before they reach the age of six. Most children remain in a learning mode. However, those that truly explode with ideas, creativity and unbounded talent are the ones introduced to knowledge in creative environments by talented and caring people. It is our responsibility as African American parents,

educators and citizens to develop educational settings—formal and informal—where cultural understandings (political, historical, literary, technological, financial, health, law, etc.) are not transmitted accidentally, but by design.[17]

Throughout this essay, the sacred music of African-American culture has been used as a theme for each section, for each motif. The songs, examples of the genius level of creative learning bestowed upon the world by the "Black and Unknown Bards" of our ancestral past, were the first pedagogical tools used to contradict the lessons imposed by the masters of slave culture. For every statement, there is a counterstatement; for every diminution of character and integrity, there is an answering call to glory and greatness. Without going into an exhaustive theoretical discussion of how the body of songs traditionally known as Negro spirituals have been used to create and sustain a culture whose collective mind was "stayed (fixed) on freedom," we can at least acknowledge that these songs—and their complementary stories, proverbs, games and sermons—were essential to the transmission of a culture that did more than react to the pathology of enslavement. Through this consciously determined establishment of African-American culture, a people who "were not beloved, became beloved." In fact they became a people, through the creative use of language, elevated to art. If we are to confront seriously the renewal of Catholic education in the service of African-American youth, then we should hear with "spiritual" ears the full implications of Sr. Thea Bowman's assertion before the National Council of Catholic Bishops in 1989:

> What does it mean to be black and Catholic? It means that I come to my church fully functioning. That doesn't frighten you, does it? I come to my church fully functioning. I bring myself, my black self, all that I am, all that I have, all that I hope to become. I bring my whole history, my traditions, my experience, my culture, my African-American song and dance and gesture and movement and teaching and preaching and healing and responsibility as gifts to the church.[18]

The catalogue of culture articulated in this portion of Sr. Thea's speech can serve as a guide for establishing any "Afrocentric" curriculum for any level of instruction. The first question to be asked is, What does the child need? Must we deposit as much canonical information as we can muster into the (perceived) empty space of the child's intellect? Or can we assume that the child, following the insight of Haki R. Madhubuti and Thea Bowman, already *knows* and *learns* on the genius level? In order for the education being suggested to take root, we must have clearly in our minds how valuable the culture of the child already is. Thea Bowman can serve as an apt example of *cultural richness,* as Frederick Douglass served us before as an example of self-generated *learning for freedom.*

Thea Bowman was placed in a Catholic school, in Canton, Mississippi, by parents who wished her to get a "good" education. At the time of her initial encounter with Catholic school systems, she was not a baptized Roman Catholic. Surrounded by a community of elders, parental figures and peers, who valued her, educated her culturally and called her to strive for excellence, she was able to absorb the best education possible at that time and place. Since her spiritual foundation had already been established, and established by black church, black community, black culture, she had a context for receiving the other information she needed—what Madhubuti refers to above as "political, historical, literary, technological, financial, health, law, etc." In the time of strict segregation, the larger community took seriously its

responsiblity to oversee and complete the education of the schools. In every class, lecture, or essay produced by Thea Bowman during her legendary life as prophet, teacher and witness, she always attributed her moral and spiritual development to the guidance of the "old folks," reminding her audiences that the triad of *church, home* and *school* was essential for her development—as well as for the development of any fully functioning, well-educated member of society.

How differently constructed was the dynamic found in the life of Frederick Douglass. His mother, whom he said he barely knew, died when he was very young, and his grandmother soon followed. Instruction—"schooling"—was of the most practical variety, and usually haphazardly rendered. The transient life he led between the ages of 4 and 14 did not allow for any sort of grounded moral instruction— except by contraries, as we have seen in his learning to seek the opposite of what his master desired. But both Douglass and Bowman sought wisdom from black elders, emphasized the hidden knowledge embedded in the content and performance of the spirituals, and, by the strictest clinical observation of reality, devised their own path of learning—based on their individual needs and on how they could be of service to the community.

Community determinants of the value of education are, therefore, of paramount importance. But if the Catholic school system can provide "by design, and not accidentally" the information, skills and methodologies necessary for young black people to survive in the world today, then a discernment must be made as to which community shall be privileged in the design of educational systems of service. True elders, in the African-American tradition, must have significant input into the curriculum of each of our schools. Grandmothers who are 39 years old, on welfare and without a history of successful child-rearing may still have the profoundest sense of the worth of an education that we can imagine. Maybe not; but a "council of elders" should be actively involved in monitoring the cultural traditions that will make a school "authentically black."

A teacher cannot teach what has not been learned. No teacher in the Catholic school system of the United States can afford to be untrained in African-American culture, especially in theology and fine arts. Children learn best when their creative skills are challenged and rewarded. "Little David, Play on Your Harp," for instance, is much more than a quaint holdover from the days of slavery. The child who is the object of the blessing in this song is being encouraged to develop musical skills (creativity); to be responsible in developing work habits ("He never would quit, 'till his work was done"); to let no seemingly impossible task become daunting ("a shepherd boy/ he killed Goliath and shouted for joy"). The song is performed (a public act); therefore the child is being praised, instructed and connected to the heroes of history—all in the course of a playful atmosphere, surrounded by adults ("significant others") who are able to be spontaneous and creative,themselves (they are singing the song), thereby modeling their lesson by their own engagement.

Hundreds of songs could be similarly used, as lesson plans incorporating all of the elements spelled out by Madhubuti and Bowman. The point here is to encourage those who would teach in a cultural setting to learn how the culture is situated. This instruction will not be mainly from lectures and calendars,and guest speakers who will be over-utilized as temporary "role models." The culture is taught through teaching creativity skills to the students. It is taught on the playground, where even the most romp-like game can teach history and ethics and spirituality. The culture springs up in verbal play, in counting rhymes and in "old time stories," spun by resi-

dents of senior homes and settlement centers. The teachers must know this culture and must learn it from the same sources, if there is to be an honest privileging of culture.

The school system, and the community that surrounds it and the Church that subsidizes it, if it is to be true to the cultural values spelled out here, must decide that no school can rest with the false goal of assimilation of its students into the larger political and economic society. As the life of Frederick Douglass, Thea Bowman, and every other African-American icon and avatar flashed before us in February will attest, the heroes of the culture sought to *transform* society, not *assimilate* into it. As long as this traditional goal of the Catholic school goes unchallenged, the result will be higher percentages of failures and increasing questions as to the continued efficacy of the presence of the Catholic school in the black community. Transformative education is another facet of *evangelization,* still named as one of the principal reasons for maintaining the Catholic school in society. Much more needs to be done, if evangelization is to move from the world of the workshop-and-certificate program into the world of crack babies, teenage parents, HIV-infected women and children, and pandemic male homicides. Leadership training is the goal, and it cannot be achieved unless a clear and ruthless assessment takes place,of the culture that is, and of the culture that needs to be. Such an assessment will not be possible if those who control the system of education still reflect inherited values, placing the highest priority on learning how "the system" works and striving to be exemplary in working the system.

Therefore, the first requirement of the Catholic school in the black community is that it tell the truth about the life conditions and expectancies of the children who are found within its walls. Once the truth has been told, then the solutions devised by many women and men of the African-American past must be applied to the recurring problems of today. If the school is to be truly Catholic, it must give utmost respect to the spirituality brought to the school by the child. Every child has a spirituality. The assault on the spirit of children, at earlier and earlier ages, causes devastations almost unimaginable to most of us—but these devastations have, in fact, been sung about for hundreds of years. Can we teach a seven-year-old orphan how to sing "Sometimes I feel like a motherless child/ a long ways from home," and then teach that child that "sometimes" is not "always," that even in that radical alienation there are choices possible for bonding and transformation? We cannot teach this lesson, or similar lessons, if we do not know how to sing the song ourselves; or if we are afraid of the raw truth contained in the song and in the circumstance. But where else can the song be sung? And by what other singers?

Too often it seems as if the fear of inadequacy stifles the effort to transform the inherited system into an opportunity for betterment. The call to conversion, of our

> ▲
> ▼
> *No teacher in the Catholic school system of the United States can afford to be untrained in African-American culture, especially in theology and fine arts.*
> ▲
> ▼

Church, our schools, our political and economic institutions begins, most powerfully, with our own personal conversion. In the passage we read earlier, from *The Price of the Ticket,* James Baldwin spoke of the process by which ethnic populations amputated part of their history for the sake of becoming white. After describing that choice, Baldwin said, in relation to Africans caught in bondage: The slave is in another condition, as are his heirs: *I told Jesus it would be all right/ If He changed my name.* If *He* changed my name.[19]

And we can understand the subtle message in the italic. Only Jesus has the right to require such a radical refiguring of the self. Our Catholic schools must fight the general cultural trend, pervasive in the United States (and in the very notion of a "new world") throughout its history: that of denying its history. Today, the pedagogical preference that has become distorted into a false discussion of multiculturalism most often means that individuals are not allowed to claim a particular ethnic identity, over and above that of any and all others. The reasoning is often thusly stated: "We will learn about all cultures in such a general way as to have no conflict or controversy." The "blanding out" of culture that then takes place has the result of trivializing all particular cultural histories. That which becomes trivialized soon disappears. Neither the rubric *conservative* nor *liberal* should dignify such a tendency. The passionate claim to a cultural identity that would be known as "Catholic" sustained several generations of men and women who desperately needed to remember "whence they came." The benefit of cultural retention helped them, we can assume, to successfully claim positions in the Church and in civil society.

African Americans have never, as a group, sought to deny their history; rather, as Douglass and others have shown us, the effort to claim a name, a place, a selfhood, an identity as a people has been the real story of black history. No better place than in the Catholic school can this be continued.

A final word, as to what should be taught in any school that would be called "black," may be offered from the writings of W. E. B. DuBois, one of the most influential learners and teachers in all of U. S. history, a man whose breadth and depth of interests and accomplishments made him as much a Catholic as any could be. DuBois wrote the following remarks on the occasion of the 45th anniversary of his graduation from Fisk University. Although the comments were written in 1933, and on the subject of "The Field and Function of the Negro College," nothing he said would not be pertinent to our meditation on the "field and function of the black Catholic school—elementary, secondary, or collegial." We should, then, read these remarks, making the necessary mental adjustments, for language.

> It is beside the point to ask whether we form a real race. Biologically we are mingled of all conceivable elements, but race is psychology, not biology; and psychologically we are a unified race with one history, one red memory, and one revolt. It is not ours to argue whether we will be segregated or whether we ought to be a caste. We are segregated; we are a caste. This is our given and at present unalterable fact. Our problem is: how far and in what way can we *consciously* and *scientifically* guide our future so as to insure our *physical survival,* our *spiritual freedom* and our *social growth?* Either we do this or we die.[20] [italics added.]

The Oblate Sisters of Providence, under the guidance of the Haitian-born Elizabeth Lange, recognized this in 1828, when they began their work of education in the black community. Henriette Delille and her associates recognized this, in 1842, when they began to care for orphans and educate black youth in New Orleans.

The orders and congregations of religious men and women who staff and subsidize the Catholic schools in the black community today still recognize the harrowing topicality of DuBois' remarks. The issue of *leadership* is the focus of his remarks, and it has been the focus of this essay and all that Catholic schools have represented—in every ethnic enclave where they have taken root.

DuBois goes on to say:

> The alternative to not dying like hogs...is [to conquer] the world by thought and brain and plan; by expression and organized cultural ideals. Therefore, let us not beat futile wings in impotent frenzy, but carefully plan and guide our segregated life, organize in industry and politics to protect it and expand it, and above all to give to it unhampered spiritual expression in art and literature. It is the council of fear and cowardice to say this cannot be done. What must be can and it is only a question of Science and Sacrifice to bring the great consummation.[21]

Spirituality and *sacrifice* should be familiar terms to those of us who learned to pray in Catholic schools. These words bring us to the final, third, motive of the Catholic school in our country: the fostering of vocations. If the deliberate nurturing of champions of justice and prophets of transformation is to be the goal of pedagogy, then we must be realistic and humble in accepting our failure to carry Catholic schooling to its inherent conclusion. Thea Bowman chose to bring her "fully functioning self" into the world of the vowed religious. Many of the (converted) men and women who are our black Catholic bishops, priests, brothers, sisters, deacons, diaconal wives, lay leaders and elders are converts to Catholicism. For many, the act of conversion was all that could have been contemplated or desired. For us, and for our tomorrows, another conversion must be more than *contemplated,* it must be *implemented.*

The Church in the black community must be transformed into a black Church, with black leadership and black authority. The model for such a church can already be found in many of our black Catholic schools. Unfortunately, the pedagogy for leadership training—for service and sacrifice within the community, within the neighborhood, within the church—has not always been a high priority. Those who were the immigrant Catholic community have benefited in myriad ways because of their Catholic instruction. The leadership and service roles the sons and daughters of these immigrants assumed carried the Catholic Church into the corridors of power and influence.

That tradition must continue. We know how to do it. We know it must be done. Little David, after all, was the greatest king Israel ever saw—and sang songs that guide us still. The question that was raised earlier in this essay, "What if educators really loved black children?" demands a way of teaching—a pedagogy—and has an answer that we do not have to journey to the top of Mount Sinai to receive. The other question before us is this: What kind of school would we organize if these children whom we love were to be called by the community to take over the leadership of this school, this parish, this city, and this were the only school available to train them?

This, too, needs no intervention or instruction from on high. We must be converted, if they are to live. There are no pagan babies anywhere, anymore. "Anybody ask them who they are, tell them they a Child of God."

NOTES

1. James Weldon and J. Rosamund Johnson, eds. *The Books of American Negro Spirituals*, New York: Da Capo Press, 1977. vol 1, p. 65. [Reprint of the 1925, 1926 editions published by the Viking Press.]

2. The recent decay of the East St. Louis public school system is vividly and poignantly portrayed by Jonathan Kozol in *Savage Inequalities: Children in Ameria's Schools* (New York: Harper Collins, 1992).

3. Scholars concerned with the education of the black child all point to how the enthusiasm for learning will fall off, alarmingly, for black children—and especially for black boys—around the period of the fourth grade. I am of the opinion, now, that a shift of spiritual strategies takes place at this time, and most educators miss the implications of such a conceptual change. More will be said of this concern, later in this essay. Some of the most cogent explanations of this phenomenon can be found in the work of Jawanza Kunjufu, especially his three-volume work, *Countering the Conspiracy to Destroy Black Boys* (Chicago: African American Images, 1985, 1986). Janice E. Hale-Benson presents an equally profound reading of this phenomenon, with abundant research data the context of her argument, in *Black Children: Their Roots, Culture, and Learning Styles* (Baltimore: Johns Hopkins University Press, 1986).

4. The two most famous examples of this phenomenon are Nat Turner, who claimed, in his "Confession," that he was given the gift of literacy by an act of God, and the mystic Rebecca Jackson, who, when her father, husband and brother denied her the possibility of learning to read and write, prayed for divine intervention. She received the gift of reading and writing after intense prayer. One presentation of Nat Turner's "Confession" can be found in *The Rhetoric of Revolution* (New York: The Macmillan Company, 1970), edited by Christopher Katope and Paul Zolbrod. The spiritual writings of Rebecca Jackson have been collected and edited by Jean McMahon Humez in the volume *Gifts of Power: The Writings of Rebecca Jackson, Black Visionary, Shaker Eldress* (Amherst: The University of Massachusetts Press, 1981).

5. Frederick Douglass, *Narrative of the Life of Frederick Douglass, An American Slave, Written by Himself* in *The Classic Slave Narratives* (New York: Mentor Books, 1987), edited by Henry Louis Gates, Jr., pp. 273-277.

6. One of the most surprising descriptions of the ethics of stealing is found in the recollections of Booker T. Washington in *Up From Slavery,* found in *Three Negro Classics* (New York: Avon, 1965), edited by John Hope Franklin.

7. Douglass, op. cit.

8. Quoted in *The Constitution and the Supreme Court: A Documentary History. Two Volumes* (Cleveland: Meridian Books, 1968), edited by Louis H. Pollak. vol. II, pp. 209-218.

9. John Dewey, *Democracy and Education* (1916), quoted in "Education and Schooling" by Mwalimu J. Shujaa, in *Too Much Schooling, Too Little Education* (Trenton: Africa World Press, 1994) , edited by Mwalimu J. Shujaa. p. 28.

10. Douglass, *Narrative*, p. 277.

11. His last mentor was William Lloyd Garrison, who taught him the techniques of abolitionism and political discourse suitable for a public life of agitation. Since Douglass met Garrison only after his escape, this relationship will not be discussed in this study.

11. Douglass, op. cit.

12. Douglass, *Narrative*, p. 297. The italics appear in the original text.

13. Douglass, op. cit.

14. James Baldwin, *The Price of the Ticket: Collected Nonfiction, 1948-1985* (New York: St. Martin's/Marek Press, 1985), pp. xix-xx. *Too Much Schooling, Too Little Education* (note #8) contains an essay which uses this insight of Baldwin as the core of its argument. See "Being the Soul-Freeing Substance: A Legacy of Hope in AfroHumanity" by Joyce E. King and Thomasyne Lightfoote Wilson, pp. 280-285. This essay should be required reading for all teachers in African-American schools, especially for the answer the authors give to the question, "What if educators really loved black children?"

15. The essay cannot review, in any detail, the hundreds of ways prejudice and denial marked the Catholic missions among the African Americans. Even those communities of men and women whose whole purpose was ministry among black people were often closed to accepting black candidates for inclusion in religious and clerical states. Cyprian Davis, O.S.B., in *The History of Black Catholics in the United States* (New York: Crossroad Publishing Co., 1991) provides a clear summary of much of the racism fostered in U. S. Catholic educational enterprises among black people. Stephen J. Oaks presents a heartbreaking story of the compromise of ministry found in the policies established to either deny or limit vocational opportunities to African-American men seeking to realize a vocation to the priesthood in *Desegregating the Altar: The Josephites and the Struggle for Black Priests, 1871-1960* (Baton Rouge: Louisiana State University Press, 1990).

16. Haki R. Madhubuti, "Cultural Work: Planting New Trees with New Seeds." Forward to *Too Much Schooling, Too little Education,* cited above.

17. In *Sr. Thea Bowman, Shooting Star: Selected Writings and Speeches* (Winona: St. Mary's Press, 1993), edited by Celestine Cepress, FSPA, p. 32.

18. After all, a 19-year-old Frederick Douglass knew enough of the glories of Western civilization to desire to be as free as any citizen of England. And many quite elderly illiterate former bondsmen and women collected their economic resources immediately after the Civil War and funded school systems across the South.

19. James Baldwin, op. cit.

20. W. E. B. DuBois, *The Education of Black People: Ten Critiques, 1906-1960.* (New York: Monthly Review Press, 1973), edited by Herbert Aptheker, p. 100.

"I have the audacity to believe that people everywhere can have three meals a day for their bodies, education and culture for their minds, and dignity, equality, and freedom for their spirit."

Dr. Martin Luther King, Jr.
Excerpt from Nobel Prize Acceptance Speech
Oslo, Norway

"Don't Let This Harvest Pass"

Evangelization and Spirituality in the African-American Catholic Experience

Therese Wilson Favors and Beverly A. Carroll

"**A**nd it shall come
to pass in the latter days
that the house of the mountain of the Lord
shall be established . . .
and all the nations shall flow to it,
and many peoples shall come and say:
'Come let us go up to the mountain of the Lord.'"
(Is 2:2)

As Pope John Paul II travels throughout the world, meeting with clergy, pastoral teams, leaders of the church and the laity in Zaire, Zambia, Uganda, India, Poland, Mexico, Eastern Europe and the United States, one message is made clear and reverberates from one country to the next: "Now is the time for a 'new evangelization.'"[1] This intensifying call for evangelization has been felt in the African-American Catholic community and is of particular interest to Catholic educators who serve in Catholic schools within the African-American community. Catholic educators question what opportunities may exist for them as they pursue this "new process of evangelization" within the school. To pursue such a process, several questions need to be addressed and discussed:

1. What is evangelization?
2. What is the school's role within the evangelization process?
3. What is the legacy of Catholic education in the African-American community in bringing people into the faith?

51

4. What are some assumptions about Catholic schools and their impact on evangelization?
5. What are the barriers to evangelization?
6. What elements relating to culture could enhance evangelization?
7. What does an evangelization program within the school look like?

This chapter aims toward discussing these questions so that Catholic educators may take advantage of the opportunities available to them in passing on the faith. Perhaps insights gained from this discussion will cause educators to intensify their efforts so that this harvest may not pass!

WHAT IS EVANGELIZATION?

So that "the word of God may run and be glorified." (2 Thes 3:1)

It would be impossible to discuss the meaning of evangelization without first understanding that it is intimately related to Jesus' ministry and the mission of the Church. The first clue in this understanding of evangelization was presented when Jesus began his public ministry. While Jesus was sitting among the elders of the Jewish community, he situated his presence and mission by quoting Isaiah: "The Spirit of the Lord is upon me, because he has chosen me to bring good news to the poor. He has sent me to proclaim liberty to the captives and recovery of sight to the blind, to set free the oppressed and to announce that the time has come when the Lord will save his people." (Is 61:1-2)

The "good news" which Jesus brought was that all of humankind was "worthy to be saved, worthy to see God and worthy to be set free from oppression." In the apostolic exhortation *Evangelization in the Modern World,* Pope Paul VI writes:

> As the kernel and center of His Good News, Christ proclaims salvation, this great gift of God which is liberation from everything that oppresses man but which is above all liberation from sin and the Evil One, in the joy of knowing God and being known by Him, of seeing him and of being given over to him."[2]

Thus, it can be concluded that evangelization is rooted in the proclamation of the good news so that individuals may experience God in a way which is liberating and leads toward personal transformation. But does this capture in its entirety the mission of evangelization, the mission of the Church?

Pope Paul VI discusses the complexities of defining evangelization:

> It is impossible to define evangelization in terms of proclaiming Christ to those who do not know him, of preaching, of catechesis, of conferring Baptism and the other Sacraments.... [This] is a partial and fragmentary definition which attempts to render the reality of evangelization in all its riches, complexity and dynamism [and] does so only at the risk of impoverishing it and even of distorting it.[3]

Pope Paul VI continues by offering another dimension to the definition of evangelization, one which includes activity aimed at the renewal of humanity: "Evangelizing means bringing the Good News into all the strata of humanity, and through its influence transforming humanity from within and making it new: 'Now I am making the whole of creation new.'" (Rev. 21:5).[4]

In the above context, evangelization takes on a twofold direction:

1. The good news must be proclaimed so that individuals may experience personal conversion;
2. This good news must be experienced in the community and in the world so that all of humanity may be transformed.

This is the twofold mission of the Church and the work of those who are disciples of Christ. Jesus reminded his disciples that true discipleship rests in the activity of spreading the good news and that this good news has the power to transform the world: 'Go out into the whole world and preach the gospel [good news] to all humankind....and believers will be given the power to perform miracles.' (Mk 16:15-17)

In simple terms, evangelization is that activity which intentionally aims at spreading the story of the Gospel to individuals and communities so that others may encounter Jesus and believe in his power to liberate and save them. As individuals encounter Christ, they become disciples of Christ, dedicated to transforming humanity with Gospel values.

What is the School's Role in Evangelizing?

"The apostles said to the Lord, 'Increase our faith!'" (Lk 17:5)

Today, the Catholic school in the African-American community serves a student body in which non-Catholics outnumber Catholics. In the 1940s, '50's and maybe some part of the '60's, the Catholic school served as the primary "keeping ground" of the Catholic faith. It was in these schools that Catholic traditions and rituals were taught and affirmed to a body of students who were predominantly Catholic. What then is the role of the school in evangelization in these changed circumstances?

The role of the school towards this new evangelization is discussed in several Church documents. Pope John Paul II says: "The ultimate goal of Catholic education is salvation in Christ."[5] This is an evangelization message which is directed to both Catholics and non-Catholics. In the African-American community, this directive is of utmost importance because Catholic schools serve so many non-Catholics and thus become the first fertile ground for "passing on the faith" to those who do not know Jesus, Catholic traditions or the sacramental life.

Additionally, the role of Catholic schools as an evangelizing agency is discussed in the document *What We Have Seen and Heard: A Pastoral Letter on Evangelization* written by the black bishops of the United States. They assert that "the Catholic school has been and remains one of the chief vehicles of evangelization within the black community."[6] As an important agent for evangelization, "these schools must be thoroughly Catholic in identity and teaching. This does not mean coercing students to join the Catholic Church, but rather to expose all the students to the religious values and teaching that make these schools unique."[7] Exposing students to the religious values and teachings of the Church will not be enough to lead people to "take a closer look" at joining the Catholic Church. The black bishops (in this same document) say this about the "new" method of evangelization, "Catholic schools in our neighborhoods should be the concern of the entire black community. As an important agent for evangelization they must be the concern even of those who have no children in the schools....In this way not a few—as experience has shown—will freely choose to investigate the Catholic faith and seek fellowship within the Catholic community."[8]

In a more recent document, *The National Congress on Catholic Schools for the 21st Century,* released by the National Catholic Educational Association, leaders of Catholic schools express these belief statements that give insight to the role of Catholic schools in evangelization:

We believe that:

- The Catholic school is an integral part of the church's mission to proclaim the Gospel, build faith communities, celebrate through worship and serve others.
- The Catholic school is an evangelizing, educational community.
- The spiritual formation of the entire school community is an essential dimension of the Catholic school's mission.
- The Catholic school is a unique faith-centered community which integrates thinking and believing in ways that encourage intellectual growth, nurture faith and inspire action.
- The Catholic school is an experience of the Church's belief, tradition and sacramental life.[9]

Since Catholic schools are established in part as agents of evangelization, "evangelizing activity" should be at the core of their existence and day-to-day operation. Catholic schools maintain a curriculum which includes religious education. In the "old days" that was enough because the students and faculty were all Catholic. Today we must go a few steps further in making the task of evangelizing distinctive from teaching.

The new evangelization would require that students and their families be directly linked with the parish community. The new evangelization would require that the parish take an active role in inviting the non-Catholic families to worship with them, to pray with them, to act with them in addressing justice issues and to fellowship with them. School leaders would be supported by parish leaders in intentional activities which lead non-Catholics, individuals and families to experience Christ in a way which forms them into disciples. This connecting of individuals to parish life so that they may experience discipleship becomes that distinctive factor which is beyond an educational experience. This connection is an integral element for successful evangelization in the school.

THE LEGACY OF CATHOLIC EDUCATION IN THE AFRICAN-AMERICAN COMMUNITY

"Wisdom has lived with us from ancient times, and generations to come will rely on her." (Sir 1:15)

Catholic education in the African-American community means that Catholic schools have provided the community with a constant reservoir of talented, educated African-American people. Without their presence, many persons serving in leadership positions, both in society and in the church, would not be there today. These schools were staffed by God-inspired educators, mostly religious women, who had a certain stubbornness when it came to learning and changing one's life.

ASSUMPTIONS ABOUT CATHOLIC SCHOOLS

The following assumptions are made about Catholic education in the African-American community:

- Catholic education still has the potential of reaching the largest number of children and families in the African-American community.
- African-American people have a deep yearning and love for the Lord and look to Catholic education to satisfy their hunger for a word of hope.
- African-American Catholic families are making a deliberately conscious effort to learn and to interpret what they learn in a way that is meaningful in the lives of African Americans.
- Catholic schools can be seen as the garden in which both religious and lay vocations are nurtured and in which devout, articulate African-American Catholics are cultivated and grown.[10]
- A demand for Catholic education appears to be growing among African Americans desiring a middle-class status for their children.
- Catholic schools provide students with a safe environment based on discipline and respect, values which are held in high esteem in the African-American community.
- Catholic schools, especially in the black community, have an important role to play in serving as sources of social outreach, of evangelization and of community support and development.[11]

Catholic schools have a long and rich legacy in the African-American community, which may be viewed as a testimony to the missionary nature of Catholic education.

BARRIERS TO EVANGELIZATION

"Clear the way in the desert for our God." (Is 40:3)

While efforts are being made to incorporate the *Nguzo Saba*, the Seven Black Principles, and Bible-based religion classes, Catholic religious instruction is primarily based on Eurocentric values and methodologies. But to be effective, Catholic education must not continue to approach evangelization in a traditionalist orientation. Before proceeding, we need to ask ourselves, What are the problems? This will set the stage for future planning and corrective action.

There are about 216,727 African-American students enrolled in Catholic schools, with approximately 80 percent being non-Catholic.[12] This shows that our Catholic schools are true to their mission and place emphasis on both racial integration and ecumenism, and that these non-Catholic families believe in Catholic education but not the Catholic faith. There are probably other barriers which could be mentioned. An effort is made here to call attention to those barriers that are most frequently mentioned.

The general perspective of parents regarding Catholic services in black parishes is that they follow an Eurocentric model. Even though the liturgy and spirituality of the Euro-American culture is changing, many traditional traits are shared, such as subdued liturgies, a personal faith in God, a rigid order of service and unemotional singing. These have become institutionalized within the Catholic educational system.

The second barrier which is most talked about is an insensitivity toward and lack of appreciation for African-American culture. As Dr. Nathan Jones has said, "Catholic educators generally fail to unravel the marvels of black cultural styles and behaviors. In short, catechists and teachers must rigorously study culture, black expressive styles and behaviors if we are ever to reverse the pattern of sterile, repeti-

tive, and maladaptive religious education modalities of faith and culture that simply don't work."[13]

Another barrier is the lack of integration between what is done in the school and what is done within the church community. Children often come home talking about the marvelous school liturgies their class designed and executed and which parents witness from time to time. But rarely are there opportunities for non-Catholic parents and families to participate in the local parish. Church activities are for church members and school activities are for parents, and never do the two meet. Very few schools and parishes have programs designed to meet the needs of the parishioners and school families. These are examples of how the Church has lost sight of its mission. The "club" mentality on either part causes an adverse reaction to building up the kingdom of God. In most Catholic parishes, one has to be a member or follow some rigid rules before participation is allowed. At one time this may have been attractive, but today it is seen as a barrier to many families and prevents them from wanting to join the Church.

But realistically, how do we invite and involve our parents in the Church? An evangelizing focus is such a new phenomenon in the Catholic Church. African-American parishes tend to be smaller and may not have a structured evangelization committee or program of welcoming. However, point persons or a connector should be made available to serve interested families.

WHAT ELEMENTS RELATING TO CULTURE COULD ENHANCE EVANGELIZATION?

'And he [Jesus] taught them in ways they understood.' (Matt 1, 4-5)

When Pope Paul VI spoke of the complexities of evangelization, he also provided insights pertaining to culture and evangelization: "Evangelization loses much of its force and effectiveness if it does not take into consideration the actual people to whom it is addressed, if it does not use their language, their signs and symbols, if it does not answer the questions they ask, and if it does not have an impact on their concrete life."[14] Therefore, some discussion regarding the culture of people of African descent is valuable to this effort of exploring evangelization in Catholic schools within the African-American community.

Father Cyprian Davis, OSB, noted theologian and historian, has identified several characteristics of black spirituality. These characteristics, once recognized and intentionally incorporated into the lifeline of the Catholic school, could enhance evangelization within the African-American Catholic school. They include the following:

Power of the word. Scripture holds an esteemed place in the spiritual life of people of African descent. It is that "praying, saving, staying power" in the black community. It is that vehicle which helps people to "wake up and see God's power." It is the story of unending love. Many African Americans see their story in Scripture: a story of overcoming, of liberation, of love. It takes on personal claim, thus becoming an individual's record of spiritual journey as well as a community's story. Scripture is an opportunity to "know who you are and whose you are."

Community-oriented. An old African proverb says, "I am because we are." Tribal living is successful in Africa because it is community-based. The community consists of families connected by blood and families connected by experience. All that is important in life is directed to the community. Thus, the spirituality of people of

African descent is community-based. We grow in our understanding of ourselves through the vast network of relationships within the community. We grow in our understanding of God through the community.

Holistic (body and soul). There is a prevailing philosophy in the African-American community that all of life is connected. Everything is connected: intellect, emotions and sentiment. Dualism does not exist because God is everywhere.

Joyful and emotional. Emotional release is common because it is an opportunity to "let go and let God." It is an opportunity to "lay your burdens down and rejoice that there is someone out there that cares and it is God." It is an opportunity to surrender to God. After all, God is omnipotent. "We are often troubled, but not crushed; sometimes in doubt, but never in despair; there are many enemies, but we are never without a friend; and though badly hurt at times, we are not destroyed." (1 Cor 8:10)

Contemplative. The opportunity to reflect and meditate on how God has moved within one's life is of special spiritual significance. It is through inner reflection that the soul may reach new heights and be healed.[15]

The above are offered because they have significance as to how evangelization is pursued in the African-American community. These characteristics are foundational for all religious education and evangelization efforts explored in the African-American community. In the words of Dr. Nathan Jones, these characteristics are "non negotiables" for sound religious education and evangelization practices. The embellishment of these characteristics will be seen in the next section, which describes a model evangelization program within a Catholic school that is connected to a parish or parishes.

What Does an Evangelization Program Look Like?

'I have come in order that you might have life, life in all its fullness.' (Jn 10:10)

Day after day, they enter into Catholic schools. They are African-American children, youth and adults. Some are Catholic, some Baptist, some AME, some Methodist, some Episcopalian and some have no church home or affiliation. But Catholic schools have always been a haven of faith, because they were built for the purpose of "passing on the faith." While the harvest looks different than it did two, three or even four decades ago, Catholic schools in the African-American community still have the resources and opportunity to invite others to "taste and see the goodness of the Lord."

Every day, the harvest of children and youth present themselves to us. Thus, every day there is a new opportunity to reap the harvest with faith. A faith that stretches back to the beginning of Christianity. A faith that has been carried by black people from the beginning with the Ethiopian eunuch and Philip. A faith from the cradle of Africa where the Church is still growing faster than on any other continent. A faith that has given us saintly people of African descent: St. Moses the Black, St. Martin de Porres, Saints Perpetua and Felicitas, Mary Elizabeth Lange, Pierre Toussaint, Henriette Delille, Thea Bowman and Archbishop James Lyke.

When families choose to send their children to Catholic schools, it must be for a reason. Perhaps in an inaudible fashion they are saying, "I want my child to have life and have it to the fullest." Isn't this what Jesus said when asked why he preached, why he taught: "I have come to give you life and give it to the fullest"? The harvest is ready. It is right in front of your eyes.

Don't let this harvest pass!

How do educators begin to be intentional in passing on the faith in a manner that evangelizes as well as educates? What role does the principal play as well as pastors, teachers and Catholic parents? How can non-Catholics be connected to parish communities? How is a climate created within the school that affirms the characteristics of black spirituality? Is there a model which could be adapted and implemented in predominantly African-American Catholic schools?

How Do We Begin the Process of Evangelization?

"Things can change in a single day; the Lord can act very quickly. If you are wise you will be careful in everything you do." (Sir 18:26)

As previous sections indicate, a connection between the parish and the school must be realized. Principals are used to organizing the resources available to execute a well-defined educational strategy for the year. In the beginning of the school year, the principal often convenes faculty and parents to discuss the curriculum and books, special events and the school calendar, fund-raisers and finances. The same should occur regarding an exploration of intentional activities for evangelization. But, an evangelization strategy is not or should not be only the principal's responsibility. Remember the new evangelization within the school requires a partnership among school faculty and parish leaders and, specifically, the parish evangelization team/committee. However, the tone for pursuing evangelization comes from the top within the school. The principal is key!

The Role of Principal Is Important

The principal is the master catechist and chief evangelist of the school's faith community. The principal sets the tone, and the spiritual climate of the school should emanate from her or his character. Priorities should be set regarding the importance of evangelization. The principal uses all opportunities to carry out the role of catechist and evangelist. The principal is to ensure that each classroom has a crucifix portraying a black Christ, a Bible and an Afrocentric decor. She or he ensures that religious devotions, prayer and praise become an integral component of the school day and the school year. The principal links the pastor and parish leaders with the students and their families and, with the pastor, links the faculty and the parish. The principal is a mighty important link! It is written in Scripture: "Who, O God, will take me into the fortified city?" (Ps 60:9) The principal has the opportunity to take an entire community into the fortified city of faith. Faith can strengthen individuals and families. Creating the right climate for evangelization and making the right connections can enhance efforts.

Creating the Right Climate

The people replied, "Who could have believed what we now report? Who could have seen the Lord's hand in this?" (Is 53:1)

The school is a place of interaction—among people and interaction of individuals with information. When one first walks into a school, one quickly observes the various levels of interaction. Evangelization can occur within these levels of interaction if the climate is right.

First, the school must portray in word and action its priority of passing on

Christian values so that disciples may be formed. As the school year begins, the principal and faculty should invite parents and students to attend a "Blessing of Teachers, Students and Parents." Grandparents and entire families are welcome, for the school is family-centered. This blessing should be held in September in the parish church, with the pastor or pastors, parish staff and elders available to participate. This signals that, above all else, the Catholic school is a community of faith, an entity of the "body of Christ" which connects consistently with the other members of the "body" through the parish. It is written in Scripture: "Revive me as you have promised." (Ps 119:25) Involve parish leaders in the planning and development of this prayer ritual, and especially the director of religious education, the youth minister and, most importantly, the parish evangelization team.

Catholic schools in the African-American community still have the resources and opportunity to invite others to "taste and see the goodness of the Lord."

Secondly, share Scripture in a consistent manner. Select a biblical quote and African proverb for each week of the school year and announce both over the public-address system. These teachings could become the spiritual and cultural vitamins for the week. Display the quote and proverb on blackboards and bulletin boards. Ask each teacher to discuss the quote from Scripture as well as the proverb. Perhaps all who are able could commit them to memory. This affirms a love for Scripture and establishes a memory bank which is both spiritual and cultural. Both the proverb and biblical quote can also be published in parish bulletins, newsletters and other forms of written communication. In this way, the parish and the school are uniting to present Scripture in a consistent manner. (The Appendix gives some suggestions for Liturgical Year B).

In addition to this gesture, obtain parish bulletins so that pertinent information about church-related activities can be passed on to all students and parents. A good resource through which to share this information is your school newsletter.

Identify members of school families who are sick and make sure their names are passed on to the parish so that these individuals will be prayed for at Sunday liturgy and are included on the list of sick and shut-ins. It is written: "I will speak out to encourage them." (Is 62:1) Make sure parents see copies of parish bulletins, even if they are not Catholic. All of this activity encourages non-believers to take a closer walk with Jesus and a closer look at the Catholic Church.

MAKING THE RIGHT CONNECTIONS: BUILDING A PARTNERSHIP WITH THE PARISH/PARISHES

"People of Jerusalem, go out of the city and build a road for your returning people." (Is 62:10)

Much of the above showcased ways to build a partnership with the pastor, director of religious education, the youth minister and the parish evangelization team/committee. However, other partnerships can and should be established.

It is important that faculties have a working relationship with parish staff and the evangelization team. Opportunities should be arranged at the beginning of the school year to interact with school families. People become interested in Jesus and interested in the Catholic Church because of the witness of people of faith. Remember, African Americans have a high regard for the extended family—the community. Therefore, the parish community should be connected with the school community. Additional ways to encourage this connection are described below.

- Ask elders of the parish to help tutor or read Bible stories to children and youth. Oftentimes the elders love to be involved with children in a one-to-one experience. These elders also could be the link in placing names from students in the bulletin for sick and shut-ins.

- Engage the director of religious education, the youth minister and the evangelization team with school faculty in developing a parish-school evangelization plan. Don't forget that the new evangelization places emphasis on the connection between non-Catholic families in the school and the parish community with parish life and activity. Together, plan at least four activities per year to achieve this goal. In every activity, establish measurable goals. The development of this plan should occur at the end of a school year so that it may be implemented in the following school year.

- Establish a working relationship between the school religion coordinator and the parish director of religious education. When these two work together, both the school and the parish benefit. They can review together curriculum materials and supplemental resources and jointly make purchases. They can share activities which have evangelization possibilities and invite families from the school to the parish and vice versa. The connection between these two staff members could enhance evangelization and religious education.

- Devise a follow-up strategy for each activity which the partnership pursues.

Sometimes the follow-up may be as simple as asking the pastor to visit a family or suggesting that the evangelization team call certain families to share news about upcoming events and to invite them to a particular church function. Evaluation of measurable objectives could also direct follow-up efforts.

Whatever the evangelization plan, the partnership between the school staff and parish leaders will make or break the success of evangelization. The partnership is the road through which people can "take a closer walk with Jesus" and take a closer look at the Catholic Church.

CONCLUSION

"Be certain in what you believe and consistent in what you say." (Sir 5:10)

This chapter's major focus was to explore the meaning of evangelization and to discuss ways to achieve it successfully. The Catholic school in the African-American community has always been held in highest esteem. It still is, largely because of the dedication and commitment of the faculty and parents. This indicates that the African-American community has faith in the Catholic educational system and a respect for the Catholic faith. Catholic schools are successful in more than one way.

Catholic schools can be even more successful in evangelization. Several insights deemed essential for evangelization to be successful in the African-American Catholic school are summarized here:

1. A paradigm shift has occured regarding an understanding of evangelization within the predominantly African-American Catholic school.
2. The new evangelization in the school necessitates a partnership with parish/parishes.
3. Parishes and schools must unite in the "formation of disciples" beyond an educational dimension.
4. Intentional activity that fosters a connection between school and parish must be done in a consistent manner for successful evangelization to occur.

God has called the Catholic school to serve as a beacon of hope within the African-American community. As the call is sent out, let us answer by teaching and preaching the good news of Jesus Christ in ways which the people can understand. Again, "be certain in what you believe and consistent in what you say"—and do it now! For the harvest is rich, and we don't want to let this harvest pass.

NOTES

1. John Paul II, *Redemptoris Missio,* December 7, 1990, #33.
2. Paul VI, *Evangelii Nuntiandi,* December 8, 1975, #9.
3. Ibid., #17.
4. Ibid., #18.
5. Pope John Paul II, address titled "Catholic Education: Gift to the Church, Gift to the Nation" given to Catholic educators at a special meeting of Leaders of Catholic Elementary and Secondary Schools and Religious Education on September 12, 1987, in New Orleans.
6. "What We Have Seen and Heard: Pastoral Letter on Evangelization from the Black Bishops of the United States," Cincinnati, OH, St. Anthony Messenger Press, 1984, p. 28.
7. Ibid., p. 29.
8. Ibid., p. 29.
9. *The National Congress on Catholic Schools for the 21st Century,* Washington, DC, National Catholic Educational Association, 1991.
10. *Lineamenta of the National Black Catholic Congress: Strangers and Sojourners No More,* New Orleans, National Black Catholic Congress, 1990.
11. Ibid.
12. Federick Brigham, *United States Catholic Elementary and Secondary Schools 1993-1994,* Washington, DC, National Catholic Educational Association, 1994.
13. Michael Talvan et al., *Faith and Culture: A Multicultural Catechetical Resource,* Washington, DC, United States Catholic Conference, 1987, p. 78.
14. Paul VI, op. cit., #63.
15. Cyprian Davis, OSB, address titled "Black Spirituality," given at the National Black Catholic Congress at Catholic University, May 22, 1987.

APPENDIX

Please note that

1. Sunday readings are from the Lectionary.
2. Proverbs can be found in
    a. *African Proverbs,* compiled by Charlotte and Wolf Leslau, White Plains, NY, Peter Pauper Press, Inc., 1962, 1982.
    b. *The House of the Heart Is Never Full and Other Proverbs from Africa,* compiled by Guy A. Zona, New York, Touchstone Books, Inc., 1993.

**Sunday's Gospel Reflections Throughout the School Year
With African Proverbs to Accompany the Theme
Cycle A/B**

	Gospel Reading	Proverb
SEPTEMBER		
Twenty-third Sunday	Matthew 18:15-20 If a brother should commit a wrong against you, go and point it out, but keep it between the two of you.	One who does what he says is not a coward.
Twenty-fourth Sunday	Matthew 18:21-35 Lord, when my brother wrongs me, how many times must I forgive him?	It is better to spend the night in irritation at an offense than in repentance for taking revenge.
Twenty-fifth Sunday	Matthew 20:1-16 God's generosity has no limits, so seek the Lord where he can be found.	What God has sent does not fail to reach earth.
Twenty-sixth Sunday	Matthew 21:28-32 We've got to have faith in someone and that someone is Jesus Christ.	Singing "Halleluia!" everywhere does not prove piety. (Ethiopia)
OCTOBER		
Twenty-seventh Sunday	Matthew 21:33-43 Use not abuse what God has given you.	The plant God favors will grow even without rain.
Twenty-eighth Sunday	Matthew 22:1-14 God will supply all your needs. Be ready when God invites you to the banquet table.	God gives nothing to those whose arms are crossed.
Twenty-ninth Sunday	Matthew 22:15-21 Give to Caesar what is Caesar's but give to God what is God's.	Two crocodiles don't live in one pond.
Thirtieth Sunday	Matthew 22:34-40 Love God, yourself and your neighbor.	Not to aid one in distress is to kill him/her in your heart.

	Gospel Reading	**Proverb**
Thirty-first Sunday	Matthew 23:1-12 Know who you follow and follow who you know—JESUS!	God gives and does not remind us continually of it; the world gives and constantly reminds us.

NOVEMBER

	Gospel Reading	**Proverb**
Thirty-second Sunday	Matthew 25:1-13 Keep your eyes open, for you know not the day or the hour.	Do well today on account of tomorrow.
Thirty-third Sunday	Matthew 25:14-30 To one who has been given much, much is expected.	It is no good asking the Spirit to help you to run if you are not willing to sprint.
Thirty-fourth Sunday Feast of Christ the King	Matthew 25:31-46 Lord, when did we see you hungry, thirsty, homeless, naked, ill or in prison?	Treat your elder as your father, your junior as your son, and your equal as your brother.
First Sunday of Advent	Mark 13:33-37 Be constantly on the watch.	When a man doesn't call, God does.

DECEMBER

	Gospel Reading	**Proverb**
Second Sunday of Advent	Mark 1:1-8 Accept the help that Jesus can give.	God does not forget the ant in its little hole (so he definitely won't for- get you).
Third Sunday of Advent	John 1:6-8, 19-28 My soul magnifies the Lord.	One who does what he/she says is not a coward.
Fourth Sunday of Advent	Luke 1:26-38 Give the gift that keeps on giving.	They who forget the aim of their journey are still on the road.
Octave of Christmas Feast of the Holy Family	Luke 2:22-40 "Rise up and rebuild your family in faith."	Don't ask me where I am going, but where I have come from.

JANUARY

	Gospel Reading	**Proverb**
Epiphany Sunday	Matthew 2:1-12 Jesus came not to save some of us—but to save all of us!	You need not tell a child that there is a God.

	Gospel Reading	Proverb
Baptism of the Lord	Mark 1:7-11 In my own Baptism, I done made my vow to the Lord.	Through others, I am SOMEBODY!
Second Sunday of Ordinary Time	John 1:35-42 Come and see someone who knows everything about you.	Hold a true friend with both of your hands.
Third Sunday	Mark 1:14-20 "Come with me," says the Lord.	A child who ask questions is not stupid.
Fourth Sunday	Mark 1:21-28 Make me a blessing, O Savior, I pray. (Jesus cures a man possessed.)	It is the place where we live that we repair.

FEBRUARY

	Gospel Reading	Proverb
Fifth Sunday	Mark 1:29-39 Take Jesus home with you so your family may be healed. (Jesus cures Peter's mother-in-law.)	Give it for the sake of God and give it to those who do not believe in God.
Sixth Sunday	Mark 1:40-45 'Tis so sweet to trust in Jesus. (Jesus heals a man).	He who has not carried your burden does not know what it weighs.
First Sunday of Lent	Mark 1:12-15 Reform your life and believe that he is, he was and that he will always be.	The true believer begins with himself.
Second Sunday of Lent	Mark 9:2-10 Teacher, how good it is that we are here. (The Transfiguration)	Travel and you will see; sit and they will come to you.

MARCH

	Gospel Reading	Proverb
Third Sunday of Lent	John 2:13-25 And then Jesus drove all of the animals and money-changers out of the temple.	What is really a load should not be called an ornament.

	Gospel Reading	**Proverb**
Fourth Sunday of Lent	John 3:14-21 Those who believe have seen a great light.	There are three friends in this world: courage, sense and insight.
Fifth Sunday of Lent	John 12:20-33 Risk life to find life.	Know how to meet and how to part.
Palm Sunday	Mark 14:1-15, 47 There comes a time in life when the situation demands more than we have.	To every field of wheat God sends its reaper.

APRIL

Easter Sunday	John 20:1-9 O Lord, how excellent is thy greatness in all the world.	I am. I can.
Second Sunday of Easter	John 20:19-31 Receive the Holy Spirit.	Anticipate the good, so that you may enjoy it!
Third Sunday of Easter	Luke 24:35-48 Why are you alarmed? God is always coming to see about YOU!	A shelter is as strong as its poles.
Fourth Sunday of Easter	John 10:11-18 Great is thy faithfulness, O God, the good shepherd!	A forest that has sheltered you, you should not call a patch of shrub.
Fifth Sunday	John 15:9-17 I am the vine, you are the branches.	Every matter of importance that is begun without the mention of God is maimed.

MAY

Sixth Sunday	John 15:9-17 "And you are my friend," says the Lord.	It is the heart that gives; the fingers only let go.
Seventh Sunday	John 17:11-19 While I was with them, I kept them safe.	Sticks in a bundle are unbreakable.
Pentecost Sunday	John 20:19-23 Be rooted in the Spirit, and YOU shall grow.	The fruit must have a stem before it grows.

Second Sunday of
Pentecost

Gospel Reading

John 1:35-42
We have found the Messiah.

Proverb

Those whom we cannot
catch, we leave in the
hands of God.

Teach All I Command.

**Legend from the Coat of Arms
of the Most Rev. Carl Fisher, SSJ
Auxiliary Bishop of Los Angeles**

"LIFT EVERY VOICE AND SING"

▲
▼

AFRICAN-AMERICAN LEADERSHIP IN CATHOLIC EDUCATION

▲
▼

DR. LORETTA M. BUTLER

While white and black clergy and religious have played and continue to play a crucial role in the lives of black Catholics, the history of black Catholics in this country places a special responsibility upon the shoulders of the laity.

These words are taken from Dr. Norman Francis' talk on "Evangelization and Black Leadership" at the National Black Catholic Symposium in 1985.

African-American Catholics have consistently contributed to the untold story of African-American Catholic education in America. In the early years of their presence on this continent, African Americans and their descendants had a unique and extremely painful beginning. Consequently, the culture of the African people, unlike that of most European immigrants, was totally disregarded. However, vestiges of a deep and profound heritage remained within the souls and hearts of the African people. These cultural roots are seen, felt and heard in their religious practices, music, song, art, dance and folklore.

In the United States, African Americans came into contact with Catholics as early as the 16th century through missionary priests in what are now California and other Western areas. In the 17th and 18th centuries, principal contact was in the proprietary colony of Maryland, where English Jesuits settled in the 1630s. Tobacco was the principal crop in the colony and the labor needed was imported from Africa, often through the Caribbean Islands. French Catholics in Louisiana also imported slaves in order to produce sugar cane.

As the majority of African Americans who would become Catholic were located in these two areas, this account of African-American leadership in education will center around events in these two former colonies. From these beginnings, educational efforts of African-American Catholics would spread into the other states as time,

conditions and events permitted.

The Catholic Church in the United States brought European traditions with it, but from the beginning it was a mission church. The Catholic bishops found it necessary to adjust and conform to American ideals and practices. Maryland, as the earliest colony of Catholic proprietors, drew upon long-standing American traditions: advocacy of the separation of church and state, a sense of civic duty and a determination to live at peace with their neighbors. Furthermore, according to Maryland's Bishop John Carroll, the first Catholic bishop in the nation, Catholics were to take a prominent role in the early government and in the financing and building of the new capital city, Washington, District of Columbia.

Slavery was another American institution. Although Catholics and other faiths baptized and educated African Americans, the condition of becoming Christian did not alleviate the legal status of their slavery. Into this climate, in which the Africans and their descendants lived, struggled and managed to survive, came educational leaders to fulfill their crucial role.

OBLATE SISTERS OF PROVIDENCE

On June 13, 1828, Elizabeth Lange, Mary Magdalene Balas and Mary Rose Boeque took residence at 5 St. Mary's Court in Baltimore, Maryland. There at the corner of the street where the first seminary for priests stood, these three women started one of the first Catholic schools for black children in the United States. One year later, in a row house on George Street, four African-American women pronounced vows, thus creating the first black Catholic religious community in the United States.

These women had arrived in Maryland as refugees from the slave revolution in the island of Hispaniola (now Haiti and the Dominican Republic). They were part of a significant influx of French-speaking refugees, many of whom were black and Catholic. One of the refugees was a Sulpician priest, Father Jacques Hector Nicholas Joubert. He had been assigned pastoral charge of the refugees and soon discovered that the children had difficulty learning the catechism. They could read neither French nor English. He approached Elizabeth Lange, who had already been operating a day school in her home, about establishing a teaching community. The teachers, who would be consecrated to God, would teach children the basic tenets of their religion.

Lange and her companions had already considered the possibility of forming a religious community, and on July 2, 1829, their dream was realized with the establishment of the Oblate Sisters of Providence. With the founding of their congregation, these educated African-American women were truly the pioneers in the long struggle to promote a Catholic education.

In 1836, their school, St. Frances Academy, opened as the only institution offering a secondary education for African-American females prior to the Civil War. Gradually, other schools were founded or staffed by the Oblate Sisters of Providence in Washington, D.C.; New Orleans; Baltimore; St. Louis; Chicago; Buffalo and other places in the United States and Cuba.

Although plagued by poverty, racism and anti-Catholic attitudes, the members persevered. They taught religion, English, penmanship, arithmetic and housekeeping skills. Although education was their major focus, the nuns also provided assistance to the poor and ill. Their efforts were not publicly commended as were other volunteers officially recognized for their services. However, other women from Haiti and

Maryland soon joined the fledgling congregation.

One woman who joined was Maria Becraft, a pioneer educator from Washington, D.C. Her father was a free black who worked as the chief steward of the famed Union Hotel in the Georgetown area of Washington. Her grandmother, also free, had worked in the household of Charles Carroll, a leading citizen of Maryland. Maria's family had sent her to the schools of Henry Potter and Mrs. Billings, white teachers who invited free children of color to study with the white children. At 15, Maria opened her own small day school for 30 girls in Georgetown in 1820. Father Van Lommel, S.J., invited her to conduct a better school opposite the convent of the Sisters of the Visitation, and this boarding and day school became the first "seminary" (secondary school) for black girls in Washington, D.C.

Teaching young black people was an act of courage, especially in 1831. That was the year of Nat Turner's slave rebellion. Because Turner was a literate black, there was tension and suspicion, and many whites wanted to see an end to black education in the South. By 1831, Maria Becraft decided to join the Oblate Sisters of Providence in Baltimore, Maryland, leaving her school in the charge of Miss Ellen Simonds, a former student.

In her life in religion as Sister Aloysius, Becraft taught French, sewing and catechism. Records show that her father sent her two sisters, Rosetta and Susanna, to St. Frances Academy in 1832, paying ninety dollars per year for their tuition. In October 1833, Sr. Aloysius became seriously ill and died on December 16 of that year. She was buried in the old cathedral cemetery in Baltimore in a section reserved for colored people. In her short life she made a truly commendable contribution to education.

Throughout their long history of service in educating African Americans, the Oblate Sisters of Providence have continued to prove that virtue and intelligence transcend race. It has been said that sanctity has no color and determination has no end. The contribution of these pioneering women to the history of the long, arduous journey to attain an education can never be adequately told.

SISTERS OF THE HOLY FAMILY

In the years before the Civil War and in spite of rigid laws prohibiting the teaching of slaves, a second religious community of African-American women was established in the Catholic colony of Louisiana. In 1842, the Sisters of the Holy Family became a reality through the efforts of free, educated African-American women, also descendants of the Haitian refugees.

Born in New Orleans, Henriette Delille met a member of a French nursing order, Soeur Ste. Marthe, who had come from France to New Orleans to work among the black poor. Delille joined her and they opened a school for free people of color. These women educated free blacks by day and gave religious instruction to slaves by night. After Soeur Ste. Marthe returned to France, Henriette met Juliette Gaudin, also a mulatto, whose parents had migrated to New Orleans from Haiti. The two young women and a third from France, Marie Jeanne Aliquot, carried on the instruction at the school.

The three women wanted to form a religious community dedicated to teaching. Their several attempts were hampered by segregation laws of the state and the prevailing attitude that only white women were called to the religious life. Finally, at the intervention of Abbé Rousselon, they obtained the support of Bishop Blanc and were

officially established as a religious congregation on the Feast of the Presentation of the Blessed Virgin Mary, November 21, 1842. They took the name of Sisters of the Holy Family. The climate of racial prejudice was such that the nuns could not take public vows until 1852 and were not allowed to wear religious clothing in public until 1872.

Education was their primary goal. Between 1848 and 1852, they opened six schools in New Orleans. Later, they opened or staffed schools in other areas of Louisiana, in Texas and in Belize, British Honduras. The group also opened the first home for African-American boys in New Orleans in 1896 and named it for their benefactor, Mr. Thomy Lafon. Lafon was an educated free black, a former teacher who became a prosperous businessman. A staunch believer in the value of an education, Lafon gave property and funds which enabled the sisters to establish St. Mary's boarding school for girls, an orphanage, and the home for orphan boys.

With Lafon's generous support and help from others, the Sisters of the Holy Family continued to evangelize and teach. In 1989, three of the sisters came to teach at Holy Redeemer School in an African-American Catholic parish in Washington, D.C. It was the first time since their founding in 1842 that members of their community witnessed God's word in the northeastern part of the United States.

Lay Catholic Leadership

The story of African-American Catholic pioneers and leaders in education in the middle years of the 19th century must include the work of laywoman Madame Marie Bernard Couvent. Her story symbolizes the drama of the African journey to America. She was born in Guinea, West Africa, and was brought to Santo Domingo, where she was enslaved. Eventually Couvent arrived in New Orleans, obtained her freedom and later married Gabriel Bernard Couvent, a free black man.

Affter her husband's death, she used the inheritance he left her to establish a free school for orphans of color in 1948. There were 250 children in attendance. An African-American lay faculty conducted classes. After the Civil War, former students and teachers of the Couvent School were among the chief leaders in the movement to create an integrated public-school system. They effectively challenged the racist assumptions about the potential of African-American children by producing graduates of outstanding accomplishments who became influential leaders in their chosen fields of endeavor.

Not all educational leadership was found within the usual classroom setting. Between 1843 and 1845, a society of colored Catholics was asserting leadership, practicing self-government and providing educational opportunities for the members of their society and their community. Father Cyprian Davis said, "one of the most precious documents for the history of black Catholics is a small notebook, 8" x 6 1/2", found in the Sulpician Archives in Baltimore. It was called the *Journal of the Commencement and of the Proceedings of the Society of Coloured People: With the Approbation of the Most Rev. Archbishop Samuel (Eccleston) and of the Rector of the Cathedral, Rev. H.D. Coskery.* This is the oldest extant written document of a black Catholic society in the United States.

This journal gives a detailed record of the weekly meetings of approximately 150-200 black Catholic men and women who met in the basement of Calvert Hall, attached to the cathedral. Meetings were held from December 3, 1843, until September 7, 1845. The members exercised self-government and made decisions

regarding their welfare and the needs of their community. They voted to name the group the Society of the Holy Family. Officers were elected and John Noel, from a prominent Haitian family, was made president. Miss Mary Holland, probably from Maryland and a descendant of the Catholic slaves who worked the tobacco plantations in Maryland, was chosen first counselor.

Despite the political foment of the years that led to the Civil War, the chief concerns of the committed lay people were their spiritual and educational welfare. Mention was frequently made of their devotional exercises, the quality of their singing, the hiring of a German professor to teach music, the concern for finances, the directions for organizing a lending library, and provision for purchasing shoes and clothing so that poor children could attend school. A list of books to be purchased included *Lives of the Saints, Poor Peoples' Catechism* and *Catholic Christian Instruction.*

Some of the members had attended the school run by the Oblate Sisters of Providence. John Noel, a successful barber, helped the sisters with their financial concerns in securing property for their school. Other members of the group helped to raise funds to further assist the Oblate Sisters. In the last pages of their remarkable journal is a financial statement revealing that the dues were 75¢ a year and the rental of the hall $2.00 per month. Each member pledged to donate $2.00 a year for the cathedral fund. This last is of interest, for it was more than a century later that black Catholics could be seated in the cathedral without restriction by race.

The leaders of this group of black Catholics realized that the key to freedom was education. Therefore, every effort was made to pursue an education for themselves and their children.

Following the upheaval of the Civil War and its aftermath, African-American Catholics became even more zealous in their striving for an education. These efforts were manifest through not only the increased activity of the two groups of religious women founded prior to the Civil War but also through

- Access to more schools, as missionary activity increased with the support of the Josephite Society and the Sisters of the Blessed Sacrament
- Continued involvement of both lay religious and women in Southern schools
- Lay Catholics confronting the crucial issues facing African-American Catholics in a segregated Church, especially through the organizations founded by Daniel Rudd and Thomas Wyatt Turner

JOSEPHITES

The call from the Catholic bishops to provide assistance to the "newly freed slaves" met with a minimum of success. However, a response to the plea came from a recently founded missionary group in England, the Mill Hill Fathers. They arrived in Baltimore in 1871. Faced with the difficulties of carrying out their missionary activities from across the ocean and increasing internal problems, they decided to form a separate order of missionaries to concentrate on the concerns of American blacks. The result of the separation was the founding of the Society of St. Joseph of the Sacred Heart, commonly known as Josephites, in 1893. They were the first and only community of religious men to dedicate themselves solely to working with African-Americans.

Prior to this, an African-American priest, Charles Randolph Uncles, was educated by the Mill Hill Fathers and ordained in 1891. He was one of the founding members

of the Josephite Society. Father Uncles, from southern Maryland, was the first African-American priest to be ordained within the confines of the United States. Discrimination in Catholic institutions had forced the few previous candidates to go to Canada and Europe for their seminary studies. Father Uncles, formed in the Josephite Seminary and ordained in Baltimore, taught at the Josephites Minor Seminary, Epiphany Apostolic College, until his death in 1933.

When they recently celebrated the first century of their ministry, the Josephite priests and brothers recounted their achievements in the establishment of 87 elementary schools and 23 high schools for African-American Catholic and non-Catholic youth. These educational efforts of white and black priests, nuns and lay persons gave hope and challenge to many young people.

One outstanding achievement was the establishment of St. Augustine High School for young men in New Orleans. In the 1944 issue of their journal, *The Josephite Harvest,* a stirring tribute is paid to George "Mike" Conner, who began his teaching career as the only African-American lay faculty member of St. Augustine in 1951. Conner taught civics, history, physical education and social studies. He also coached basketball, football and track. A native of Baldwin, Louisiana, he had received his education in Catholic schools founded by the Sisters of the Blessed Sacrament in New Orleans. These were Blessed Sacrament Elementary School, Xavier Prep and Xavier University. Conner pioneered in the integration of African-American schools into the Louisiana High School Athletic Association. His community activities included membership in the Louisiana State Legislature from 1972 to 1984 and service on the committee on education and on other local and national committees.

SISTERS OF THE BLESSED SACRAMENT

Founded in 1981 by Blessed Katharine Drexel of Philadelphia, the congregation was dedicated to the education of Native Americans and African Americans. Drexel realized, as did the African-American religious community founders who preceded her, that the hope for the future of African Americans was through access to quality education.

Two of the earliest efforts of the Blessed Sacrament Sisters were in Virginia. St. Emma's Industrial and Agricultural Institute, founded in 1895, was the only African-American military high school in the United States. One of the graduates recently wrote of a reunion of his class in 1969. The writer, Michael A. Smith, noted that St. Emma's had the ability to turn misguided and confused youth around while enhancing the skills of the gifted. He had come from an inner-city neighborhood in Washington, D.C., in 1966. At that time there were in the school 300 cadets from every major city in the United States, the Caribbean and Africa. High academic standards were upheld in an atmosphere of strict discipline and respect. In the early 1990s Mr. Smith wrote of a plan to revive the spirit of St. Emma's and its sister school for girls, St. Francis de Sales (opened in the 1890s), by negotiating with the owners of the grounds of old St. Francis. The future goal of the alumni is to establish a new school to be called the Virginia Center for Science and Mathematics.

Thirty-four years after the opening of St. Emma's in 1925, the Sisters of the Blessed Sacrament built the capstone of their long list of education efforts for African Americans, Xavier University of New Orleans. This university is the first and only historically African-American Catholic coeducational university in the United States. Through this institution, the sisters provided a quality education for minority stu-

dents who were turned away from established Catholic colleges and universities. At Xavier University, students received excellent academic training in fields where they were not then welcome. When its graduates went out into communities anywhere in the nation, they filled the classrooms with teachers, staffed the pharmacies, became social workers, scientists, doctors, lawyers, artists in every medium, judges, presidents of colleges, superintendents of schools, civil rights leaders, theologians and achieved every other vocation to which they were called.

The president of Xavier University for over a quarter century, Dr. Norman Francis is also a graduate of Xavier University. As an African-American Catholic educational leader deeply involved in community concerns, he has been an adviser to four United States presidents.

In an address, "Evangelization and Black Leadership," given at the first National Black Catholic Symposium held in 1985 in Detroit, Dr. Francis noted the "wealth of indigenous talent" in the black Catholic community. "Education," he further stated, "is essential to black progress in the Church as well as in the secular world." He called special attention to the creation of the Institute for Black Catholic Studies, just beginning at Xavier. The institute was to be the site for discernment of the relationships of Vatican II and the social encyclicals to the black Catholic community. It would stress the development of Catholic appreciation for black cultural expressions for more effective ministry to black Americans. Today the institute continues to train and nurture black and white Catholic leaders for effective ministry among African Americans.

EDUCATIONAL EFFORTS IN THE SOUTH

There is a long-overdue chapter in the history about the perseverance of African Americans to teach in spite of the odds. One of those who persevered in the rural Catholic schools of southwestern Louisiana is a lay woman, Eleanor Figaro. In 1916, Figaro, a graduate of St. Paul's School, gathered 18 children in a shed and began the first Catholic school for African Americans in Lafayette, Louisiana. She later taught at Sacred Heart School for 42 years and in 1949 became the first African-American woman to receive the papal honor *Pro Ecclesia et Pontifice.* She is only one of the known and unknown educators across the nation who have made it possible for African-American Catholics to pursue their dreams.

Many of these dedicated persons did not receive awards or achieve fame. One extraordinary educational pioneer was Mother Mathilda Beasley. She was born about 1833 in New Orleans. Her mother was a Creole of color and her father a Native American. One account reports that Mathilda Beasley risked imprisonment for instructing slaves and free black children in Savannah, Georgia.

After going to England to become a religious sister, she returned to Georgia and established a small community of Franciscan Sisters. After suffering many trials and the lack of financial support, the order was suppressed in May 1985. Mother Mathilda decided to give up her dream of a religious congregation. Instead, she lived alone in a small house provided by Father Oswald Moosemuller near Sacred Heart Church, a church which had been built for black Catholics. She devoted her earnings from sewing to charity. Mathilda Beasley died December 20, 1903. The witness of her life and the efforts she made on behalf of orphans indicate that she was a woman of great faith and deserves an honored position in the history of African-American Catholic

educators.

The difficulties encountered by Mother Mathilda Beasley in Georgia provide more insight into the types of problems confronting African-American Catholic education in the early 20th century. Yet within two decades, the third successful community of African-American women religious was founded in Savannah, Georgia, in 1916 by Father Ignatius Lissner, who proposed a community of black sisters to be called the Handmaids of Mary.

Father Lissner received the support of an African-American woman, Elizabeth Barbara Williams. Born in 1868 in Baton Rouge, Louisiana, she spent some time in a community of black sisters which was later suppressed. She then went to the Oblate Sisters of Providence in Baltimore. After leaving the Oblates, she worked as a receptionist at Trinity College in Washington, D.C. There Lissner contacted her and persuaded her to become the foundress of a religious community. She yielded to his appeal and became known as Mother Theodore Williams. After difficult times in Savannah, Mother Theodore decided to move her young community to New York, and, at the invitation of Cardinal Hayes, the community settled in Harlem in 1922. There they conducted a day nursery, established a day nursery, established a soup kitchen, taught kindergarten and cared for homeless children. In 1929, the community affiliated with the Franciscans and became the Franciscan Handmaids of the Most Pure Heart of Mary.

Despite initial trials, the community flourished and began to staff parochial schools such as St. Benedict the Moor in Manhattan and St. Aloysius in Harlem. The group numbered 20 at Mother Theodore's death in 1931. Through the years, their work has been carried on in other parts of the United States and in the Caribbean islands; however, their main educational mission remains in Harlem.

LAY LEADER DANIEL RUDD

In the absence of a representative African-American clergy until well into the 20th century, educated Catholic laymen fulfilled the much-desired role for national leadership. Several issues needed to be addressed at these crucial times in African-American history. One lay leader of the group in the late 19th century was Daniel Rudd.

Daniel Rudd was born a slave on August 7, 1854, in Bardstown, Kentucky, of Catholic parents. Following the Civil War, Rudd moved to Springfield, Ohio, where he received a secondary education. In 1866 he founded a newspaper called the *Ohio State Tribune*. In that same year he changed the focus of the weekly publication and renamed it the *American Catholic Tribune*. On the editorial page were the words "The only Catholic journal owned and published by colored men." His staff wrote articles on the serious national problems confronting black people both within the Catholic Church and in the American mainstream. These problems included racial discrimination, lack of representation in Catholic organizations and the lack of comparable access to education.

Besides publishing the paper, Rudd made history with his idea to call a national black Catholic congress. His aim was to bring together African-American Catholic lay leaders from around the nation for mutual support and to serve as spokepersons for the alleviation of the problems and issues. Rudd's dream became a reality when the first of five congresses was held in Washington, D.C., from January 1-4, 1889. Meetings were held in St. Augustine Church, the oldest Catholic church established

by African Americans in the city. Mass was celebrated by Father Augustus Tolton, and the sermon was delivered by Cardinal James Gibbons. The newspaper stated that 200 delegates attended this first congress. Elected president, Daniel Rudd suggested the need for schools, for training in labor skills, for family values. Other addresses were given, outlining the needs and possible solutions to the issues of deep concern.

The second congress was held in Cincinnati on July 8-10, 1890; the third, in Philadelphia in 1891; the fourth, in Chicago in 1893, and the last one held in the 19th century was in Baltimore at St. Peter Claver Church in 1894. The concern for education was the dominant theme at each of the five congresses. At the last one a prominent delegate, Dr. William S. Lofton, insisted upon the creation of a national Catholic institution to meet the intellectual, manual and industrial needs of African-American youth. This urgent plea was finally realized in the establishment of the Cardinal Gibbons Institute in Ridge, Maryland, in 1925.

The Cardinal Gibbons Institute was founded under the direction of the Jesuit priest Father John La Farge. He had been the priest of St. Peter Claver Parish, an African-American parish in Ridge. After many delays, including World War I, the institute became a reality and two prominent African-American educators, both graduates of Tuskegee Institute in Alabama, Victor Daniel and his wife Constance, guided the school as principal and assistant principal. Courses in academic and industrial subjects were offered for the coed high school student body. Financial problems and the economic depression caused the school to close in 1933. It reopened in 1937 and continued operating until 1967.

Lay Leader Thomas W. Turner

The work for justice for African Americans was ably led by Dr. Thomas Wyatt Turner, a black Catholic from infancy and a native of Hughsville, Maryland, in Charles County. Born in 1877, Turner received his secondary education at a black Episcopalian school and then went to Howard University, where he studied to be a teacher of biology. After teaching at Tuskegee Institute and at high schools in Baltimore and St. Louis and pursuing postgraduate studies, he received a master's degree from Howard and a doctorate from Cornell in 1921.

Teaching was his career, but working for civil rights became a lifelong passion. After working in local and national organizations, he began placing his greatest emphasis on racial discrimination within the Catholic Church. His efforts led to the formation of the Federated Colored Catholics in 1925. Its first meeting, like that of the first lay congress in 1889, was held at St. Augustine Church in Washington, D.C. This national group of committed, well-educated laymen was active in confronting the Catholic Church regarding its responsibility to provide justice for its African-American members. Correspondence to the Church officials and to Rome was sent annually. Lists of grievances were brought to their attention forcefully. Much was accomplished and much was left to be done by others. Dr. Turner and his group continued to fight the battles to change the unjust systems. His achievements in a long life of sacrifice in the pursuit of justice through education are a challenge for everyone.

Events in the mid-20th century provided opportunities and challenges for all Americans in every aspect of their lives: moral, political, economic and, particularly, educational. Many events caused upheavals in the public arena that are still rever-

berating and have impacted Catholic education for African Americans. Chief among these events were the following, some of which are discussed in more detail:

- Migration from rural to urban areas
- *Brown vs. Board of Education* decision regarding reverse discrimination in higher education
- Bakke decision regarding reverse discrimination in higher education
- Civil Rights Movement of the 1960s
- Open-space concept in education
- Vatican II
- Changing public policy regarding affirmative action
- Increased black middle class, with subsequent exodus of blacks from urban areas in the 1980s and 1990s and the economic and moral decline of cities
- Merger and consolidation of urban Catholic schools
- Renewed interest in Afrocentric education
- Decline in religious staffing of schools
- The Coleman Report and other studies reporting the positive impact of Catholic education on the achievements of African Americans

The 1954 *Brown vs. Board of Education* decision, which outlawed segregation in public schools, also affected the policies of the Catholic school systems in the nation. Some diocesan school systems had integrated their schools prior to the momentous decision. Many schools in rural areas, especially those under the jurisdiction of religious orders, had to close or be placed under diocesan control. Among them were schools in St. Louis; Wheeling, West Virginia and Washington, D.C. African-American Catholics and non-Catholics had migrated to large cities such as Los Angeles, Chicago, New York, Philadelphia, Detroit and Washington, D.C.

One of the secondary schools founded in the inner-city of Los Angeles in 1962 was Verbum Dei. This school, administered by the Society of the Divine Word, was founded to meet the needs for a quality secondary education in South Central Los Angeles. The first principal was Father Joseph Francis, now (retired) auxiliary bishop of Newark, New Jersey. With a tradition of parent and community involvement, the school is an oasis in the city and has become a leading educational institution. With the religious dimension as the cornerstone of its strong academic program, over 70 percent of Verbum Dei graduates have entered college to prepare for successful careers.

Another city high school established in 1962 is Hales Franciscan in Chicago, founded by the Franciscan Fathers for young men. As one of the few predominantly African-American all-male schools in the United States, it has succeeded in preparing the youth so that more than 90 percent are accepted into colleges and universities. A strict academic environment is maintained, a dress code is enforced, and involvement with drugs and gangs is forbidden. Rev. Charles E. Payne, the school's first African-American president, takes the school's mission very seriously. He says that the school provides academic training in an environment that allows the young men to feel secure about themselves and their responsibilities.

These two institutions and many others around the nation provide the opportunities for African Americans to receive a Catholic education and are gradually becoming more accessible. Many Catholic organizations are evolving, and through seminars, conferences, workshops and other means, concerns are being faced and solutions recommended. Nevertheless, there is still a need for more African-American

school administrators to implement the tremendous responsibilities of running large archdiocesan systems. Representation of African Americans has been very limited.

In the 1980s the Archdiocese of Washington, D.C., appointed Dr. Katherine W. Cole as the first African American to assume the duties of secretary for Catholic education in the archdiocese. More recently, Dr. Sandra N. Smith was appointed in 1992 as assistant director/superintendent for Catholic education and the office of child/youth ministries in Milwaukee. Dr. Smith had a long and very successful career as an associate professor of education at Howard University in Washington, D.C., and served for 24 years as a director of religious education for a Washington, D.C., parish. In the late 1980s she was appointed the first lay principal of Bishop McGuiness Memorial High School in Winston Salem, North Carolina, from which she had graduated in 1952. Dr. Smith became a Catholic in 1960 and attributes her love for the faith to the Sisters of St. Francis, who taught her in the elementary school years.

In the future there must be a conscious effort to ensure the presence of qualified African-American Catholic educators and administrators at every level, along with special and conscious efforts to preserve the highest quality and affordable parochial schools in areas near predominantly African-American neighborhoods and centrally located Catholic high schools. The following strategies can help to achieve these goals:

There must be a conscious effort to ensure the presence of qualified African-American Catholic educators and administrators at every level in parochial schools near predominantly Afrian-American neighborhoods.

- African-American parents, educators, business persons and others must be involved in every decision-making process available regarding Catholic education.
- African-American Catholic educators and administrators must be recognized and actively recruited.
- New pools of African-American teachers, retired teachers and internships for college students must be considered.
- Colleges where African-Americans are predominant, such as Xavier University of New Orleans, Hampton University and Howard University, should be visited.
- The needs of African-American families must be included as public relations efforts are created for the Catholic schools.
- Scholarship incentives must be provided through service in Catholic schools and recruitment of high school seniors for pursuit of degrees in education and administration.
- Catholic education for African Americans must include the contributions of all cultures through a balanced presentation in the curriculum.
- Ways must be found to attract and retain African-American teachers in Catholic schools.

- The contributions of dedicated African-American Catholic educators, past and present, as evidenced by their graduates should be utilized.

As the 21st century approaches, the challenges of the future for African-American Catholics will be met with the faith and fortitude of the pioneers who preceded them. What are these challenges and how will they be addressed?

It may be well to reflect on the words of the late Sr. Thea Bowman, teacher, singer and consultant for intercultural awareness at the Xavier University Institute for Black Catholic Studies and the Diocese of Jackson, who said in an address to the bishops in July, 1989:

> ...I come to my church fully functioning. I bring myself, my black self, all that I am, all that I have, all that I hope to become. I bring my whole history, my traditions, my experience, my culture, my African-American song and dance and gesture and movement and teaching and preaching and healing and responsibility as gift to the church.[1]

Finally, the black Bishops of the United States, in "What We Have Seen and Heard," a pastoral letter on evangelization, have written:

> African American spirituality is based on the Sacred Scriptures. In the dark days of slavery, reading was forbidden, but for our ancestors, the Bible was never a closed book. The stories were told and retold in sermons, spirituals and shouts.[2]

NOTES

1. In *Sr. Thea Bowman, Shooting Star: Selected Writings and Speeches* (Winona: St. Mary's Press, 1993), edited by Celestine Cepress, FSPA, p. 32.

2. "What We Have Seen and Heard: Pastoral Letter on Evangelization from the Black Bishops of the United States, Cincinnati, OH, St. Anthony Messenger Press, 1984, p. 4.

SELECTED BIBLIOGRAPHY

Butler, Loretta M., "A History of Catholic Elementary Education of Negroes in the Diocese of Lafayette," Louisiana, Ph.D. Dissertation (1963).

Davis, Cyprian, OSB, *The History of Black Catholics in the United States* (1990).

Devore, Donald E. and Joseph Logson, *Crescent City Schools* (1990).

Gasperetti, Elio, Marilyn Nickels, and Anthony Scally, *African Heritage in the Catholic Church* (1979).

Gerdes, Sr. Reginald, OSP, "To Educate and Evangelize—Black Catholic Schools of the Oblate Sisters of Providence (1828-1880)," *U.S. Catholic Historian,* vol. 7, nos. 2 & 3, Spring-Summer, 1988, pp. 183-199.

Hennessey, James, *American Catholics: A History of the Roman Catholic Community in the United States* (1978).

Hogan, Rev. Peter, "Josephite History," *The Josephite Harvest* (1992-1993).

Holy Family Sisters, *The Greatest Gift of All: A Pictorial Bibliography of Mother Henriette Delille, Foundress of the Sisters of the Holy Family* (1992).

Interview of Sandra Noel Smith in *The Catholic Herald,* Milwaukee, WI, Feb. 13, 1992.

Sherwood, Grace H., *The Oblates' One Hundred and One Years* (1931).

Smith, Michael Alexander, "St. Bootstraps—Why D.C.'s Young Black Kids Need the Tough Love We Knew at Military School," *The Washington Post,* January 9, 1994, p. C5.

Spaulding, D., "The Negro Catholic Congresses," *Catholic Historical Review* (1969).

Sulpicians of the Archdiocese of Baltimore, Record Group 41, Box 1, Oblate Sisters of Providence, *Journal of the Society of Colored People.*

The Catholic Standard, Archdiocese of Washington, July 13, 1989, p. 14; December 29, 1994; February 2, 1995; January 14, 1995.

The Josephite Harvest, vol. 97, no. 2, Summer 1994, p. 1.

U.S. Catholic Historian, "The Black Catholic Community" (1988) and "The Black Catholic Experience" (1986).

Verbum Dei, Silver Anniversary 1962-1987, Los Angeles, CA.

Warnagiris, Sr. M. Clare, "Maria Becraft and Black Catholic Education (1827-1832)," M.A. Thesis, Morgan State College (1974).

MODEL SCHOOLS

▲
▼

BEVERLY A. CARROLL

We could not possibly list all of the schools in different parts of the country that are doing wonderful work in the African-American community. This is just a sample of interesting things that are being done.

Changes have taken place in Catholic schools to accommodate a diverse population of students. This section is the result of a search for models whose programs relate to African-American children. While many others exist, the following schools were chosen as a result of responses to our research.

Catholic schools have a rich history of educating African-American youth. Catholic schools in urban areas have always taken pride in their mission to both educate and proclaim the Gospel of Jesus Christ to the poor and underserved. The rise in costs and dwindling funds for education have particularly impacted a number of inner-city Catholic schools, causing many to shut down. This trend has echoed across the country.

Despite many closings, there are Catholic schools that have kept their doors open. They are marching into the third millennium with a new beacon of hope. In the African-American Catholic school community there already exist successful models for educating African-American children. There are exciting and innovative ideas being used to successfully educate and meet the needs of African-American youth and families. We looked at teaching strategies, structure of the school curriculum, resources available and the networks involved in the programs' success.

The following are monographs of five such schools. Some have been in existence for many years. Others are brand new. Their program outcomes include the enhancement of the African-American child's ability to learn, improved school behavior, accelerated overall school performance, good citizenship and leadership skills, and increased college acceptances. It is hoped that these innovative ideas will serve as models of success in education for the future.

ST. ALOYSIUS SCHOOL—HARLEM, NEW YORK

St. Aloysius School flourishes in the Central Harlem community. St. Aloysius School was founded over 50 years ago by the Franciscan Handmaids of Mary, one of the three orders of African-American sisters in the United States. In 1985, the responsibility for the school was assumed by the Jesuits. A new role for the school

was patterned in response to the educational crisis facing inner-city children after an assessment was done. A new and innovative program was created which focuses its attention on the family as well as the educational needs of each child. The school's mission is to empower students with an appreciation for their culture and to assist them in building confidence in themselves and their abilities today and with vision to the future. Special emphasis is placed on academic excellence, the formation of a strong value system and concern for developing positive relationships.

With a current enrollment of 208 students, there are three programs to serve grades pre-K through 8: 1) The Mother Theodore Program - a coeducational pre-K and kindergarten program that is creative and nurturing, with emphasis on academic preparation, creativity, cognitive learning, language development and socialization skills. 2) The Pierre Toussaint Program - a coeducational elementary school program that places emphasis on fostering integrity and personal responsibility and on academic skills development. The school day is lengthened by 45 minutes to offer a wider range of activities, including foreign language and creative arts. The traditional curriculum is supplemented by school trips to libraries, museums and cultural events. 3) The Gonzaga Program—a middle-school program for boys only, ages 11-14, that addresses the special needs of boys, emphasizing the development of personal relationships, academic achievement and leadership skills. It has a predominantly male faculty who present a challenging curriculum to prepare students for admission to the Catholic high schools and for their continued success once enrolled. All students receive computer instruction through the Courage to Succeed program. Through this program, students are exposed to the life and career experiences of many of the metropolitan area's most influential African-American and Hispanic business leaders.

The Sister Thea Bowman Program is proposed. It is designed to maximize the potential of junior high school-aged girls. In addition to a superior academic curriculum, it will address the special problems faced by young women today, such as vulnerability to abusive relationships, teen pregnancy, physical violence and substance abuse. The goal is to improve self-esteem, foster personal empowerment and prepare young women to meet the educational and professional challenges ahead.

At St. Aloysius, parents play an important and direct role in their children's education. There are regular teachers conferences, individual consultations, monthly family nights and parent-education programs. St. Aloysius School's value-based curriculum and philosophy, developed in tandem with members of the community, represent a singular opportunity to help youngsters grow towards productive adulthood. They challenge students to be different from what they see on the streets of Harlem and to have an impact beyond the school walls. An increased enrollment has been a good indicator of how well the school has been doing.

St. Benedict's Preparatory School—Newark, N.J.

Born out of the 1967 riots in Newark, St. Benedict's, an all-male school, was reopened in 1973 to educate mostly African American males from the inner-city. The school has been in existence for a total of 125 years. Fr. Edwin Leahy, with a handful of Benedictine monks, decided to stay in Newark after the riots and built the once mostly all-white school into a model program. The mission of St. Benedict's is to provide a strong academic program and high standards of responsibility, honesty and integrity to young men who come from an area where there are few reasons for hope.

Today, there are 522 students enrolled in grades 7-12. Sixty-six percent are African American. The school runs 11 months of the year, with August off. The school accepts the average student as well as the A student. Good discipline is a requirement for admission. Freshmen start with a week of basic training, sleeping in the school and getting to know how St. Benedict's works. The same "classical" college preparatory program that was always used at St. Benedict's is still used. There is a four-year African-American history course. The result is that 95 percent of St. Benedict's graduates go on to college, compared to the national average of 30 percent. Such prestigious colleges attended include Morehouse, Hampton, Morgan, Harvard, Columbia and Cornell. Among many scholarship and mentoring programs involved with the young Black men at St. Benedict's are INROADS and Tribute to Young Black Men, Inc. St. Benedict's is the only New Jersey member in the National Network of Complementary Schools, a group of 30 high schools in the U.S., Canada and the Virgin Islands that exchange pupils on a voluntary basis.

St. Benedict's boasts of its prized, bright and well-prepared minority males and is a prime feeder school to the best Catholic colleges in the country as well as to Ivy League schools. Its programs include a better understanding of history and culture as well as its leadership training for young men. St. Benedict's Preparatory is a model program.

The proposed Sister Thea Bowman Program is designed to maximize the potential of school-aged girls.

CORNERSTONES—DETROIT

Cornerstones is a triad of three new coed schools in the Detroit area. The project is an ecumenical effort of several ministries, including the Catholic, Episcopalian, Lutheran, Baptist and non-denominational churches, in partnership with the corporate world. The Archbishop of Detroit financially supports the Cornerstones project, whose mission is 1) to increase the opportunities for quality education; 2) to increase opportunities for school completion; 3) to increase opportunity for future employment and 4) to impact the family in faith and in the community.

The Cornerstones Schools opened in 1991. Children from every faith attend. The Gospel is the thrust. There is a rigorous academic program that runs for 11 months of the year, instead of the traditional ten. With permission from Cardinal Adam Maida of Detroit, Dr. Norma Henry, who serves as the associate superintendent for Catholic schools in the archdiocese of Detroit, is on leave from the archdiocese to serve as director of the Cornerstones Schools.

There are two schools on the east side of Detroit for grades kindergarten through 5. On the west side is the middle school, grades 6, 7 and 8. Ninety-seven percent of the students are African American.

The curriculum is based on the fundamentals of writing, reading, mathematics, science, and reasoning, integrated with a strong foundation of moral development and character education. The teachings are not focused on any one religion, but on Gospel values, the teachings of Christ, the belief in loving one's neighbor and the

concept of knowing Christ in daily life. Parents play a big role. They must sign a "covenant," an agreement to support the school and be active in meetings, parent/teacher conferences and homework supervision. Students eight years old and older also sign the agreement.

The growing number of students, test results and community feedback are indicators of the schools' success thus far. The Cornerstones Schools hope to be a part of change; to tap into and unleash the potential that they believe God has given each student.

Private corporations provide funding for the project and professionals serve as mentors for the youth. Dr. Henry boasts that the youth are doing quite well on standardized achievement tests.

The schools' doors are open to everyone on a first-come, first-served basis. There are no admissions tests. The schools started with 145 students and now have 407.

Cardinal Ritter High School—St. Louis

Cardinal Ritter High is located in northern St. Louis, Walnut Park to be exact, a high-crime area that does not lend itself to success of young adults. Now in its 16th year, Cardinal Ritter has a coed student body of 300 in grades 9-12. It is 100 percent African American. Its mission is to foster academic excellence and leadership development. The school was run by the Jesuits in the past, but the mostly lay faculty today has one part-time woman religious. There are currently no priests. There are more male faculty members than female, and a number of them are African-American male teachers.

Mrs. Carmele Hall, who is president and principal, believes that everyone who walks through the door is a leader: "You just have to develop that, and our faculty goes the extra mile."

In addition to the college preparatory curriculum, there are a variety of activities, including peer tutors, student ambassadors and a mentoring program. The Simba Group (Young Lions) is an African-American history and culture study group. African American history, literature and drama are a part of the curriculum. Each year, faculty select 50 students to participate in a two-day leadership conference, where they look at what influences them as leaders. As a result, they develop ideas that will impact upon their school and the community. The rest of the year is spent implementing the ideas.

Ninety-five percent of the graduating seniors attend college and qualify for scholarships. The training from Cardinal Ritter not only prepares students to be successful in high school, but looks beyond to assure success in college.

"Our students don't skip school," says Hall. "You'd think we have an extended-day program because the students stay long after classes are over to use the library and participate in various activities." The school recently added a state-of-the-art writing skills laboratory and math lab for incoming students. There is a tutoring program three days a week which teachers run. Students who are at risk are asked to participate, but anyone is welcome. "Parents," says Hall, "are very involved." Cardinal Ritter has a very high graduation rate. "I believe in this school. Some call it a beacon in the community."

The emphasis on leadership as well as on history and culture empower African-

American students at Cardinal Ritter for success in the future. The success of every student is considered to be an indication that the school's mission is being accomplished. Emphasis on the individual makes this a model in education.

ST. FRANCES ACADEMY—BALTIMORE

St. Frances Academy is located in the Johnson Square neighborhood of Baltimore, where there are many young people who are not prepared for high school academically or emotionally.

There are 175 African-American students in grades 9 through 12 at St. Frances. A quarter of the students live with a guardian, foster parent or grandparent; another quarter come from two-parent homes, and half come from single-parent homes. Previously an all-girls academy, St. Frances became coed in 1974. It was also once a boarding school with an international population.

"Our student body is diverse. We have the average kid, those who are bright and those with difficulty. The only ones we turn down are those who don't want to come. If they can do the work or if there is potential to be able to do it at some point, we take them," says Sr. John Frances Schilling, OSP, who has been principal for two years. "We have kids who come from special education in other schools who make the honor roll here!"

Staffed by eight Oblate Sisters of Providence, a Franciscan and three Christian Brothers, St. Frances Academy, now in its 165th year, is finding new ways to educate its students. Two new programs were installed in 1995. St. Frances has extended the school day to nine periods to include a course for males called Boys to Men. The program emphasis is on communication skills, bonding, people skills and talk about black wealth and entrepreneurship. Sisters, the girls' component to the program, covers such areas as relationships, self-esteem building and sisterhood.

The school has also entered into a three-year partnership with the Community Partnership for Education Task Force and the business community to prepare students for the business world. The partnership members include the Archdiocese of Baltimore, Baltimore City Public Schools, banks, local businesses and a Baptist church. The program will be an in-service program to work on team building, conflict resolution and teaching students accountability. There will be a parenting center for parent involvement as well.

The first phase of teacher training includes a five-day workshop to talk about the school's curriculum and what is needed to prepare students for the work world. In 1996 the curriculum will be put in practice and the third year will be an evaluation year. If the program works, it will be replicated in other schools, and it is hoped that it will attract other businesses to participate.

Afterword

Most Rev. John H. Ricard, SSJ

The publication of these five essays under the title *'Rise 'n' Shine: Catholic Education and the African-American Community'* is an innovative attempt to examine Catholic education from the perspective of the African American Catholic experience. The areas addressed include insights from such areas as pedagogy, catechetics, history and culture, and leadership development.

This publication comes as a welcomed addition to the previous volumes on Catholic schools in the United States published by the National Catholic Educational Association. Its focus on the African-American presence in Catholic education enriches some of the well-developed reflections as African Americans themselves enrich the Catholic Church. Written from a variety of perspectives in a clear, incisive and forceful manner, the chapters herein present an impelling contribution to our understanding of the role of the Catholic schools and parish religious education programs.

The authors also remind us that African Americans have been present in Catholic schools since their beginnings in this country. This is an important observation, as it challenges the popular myth that Catholic schools were on the periphery and did not play a substantial part in the development of education among African Americans. Today, African Americans strongly endorse and affirm the initiatives taken by many dioceses to develop creative and imaginative ways of providing the continued moral and financial support of Catholic schools.

One cannot but observe that the authors write with a degree of passion and conviction found in publications of this sort. Their remarks celebrate and affirm the invaluable contributions of Catholic schools and parish religious education programs to the African American community, and one reads between the lines a subtle plea for their continuance.

Finally, the authors underscore the continued challenge that must be faced if Catholic schools in the African-American community are to continue, that is, exploring models which exist in several dioceses for financing schools in depressed neighborhoods; effective methods of catechesis and religious instruction in parish religious education programs and schools which have a predominantly non-Catholic enroll-

ment; and ways in which Catholic schools can be effective vehicles for evangelization and a force for community development and neighborhood stabilization.

The entire Catholic community owes a debt of thanks to the authors and to NCEA for providing the initiative and resources for this important project. It is hoped that this modest beginning will mark a new phase of growth and development of Catholic education in the African-American community.

Most Rev. John H. Ricard, S.S.J.
Auxiliary Bishop of Baltimore